BALLS!!

BALLS!!

 A–Z of
Football's Funniest Stories

Ronnie MacKay

BLACK & WHITE PUBLISHING

First published 2010
by Black & White Publishing Ltd
29 Ocean Drive, Edinburgh EH6 6JL

1 3 5 7 9 10 8 6 4 2   10 11 12 13

ISBN: 978 1 84502 328 7

Typeset by Ellipsis Books Ltd, Glasgow
Printed and bound by MPG Books Ltd, Bodmin

Contents

Acknowledgements

Thanks to all those who have been part of the A to Z institution – and long may it continue. Also thanks to my better half Janey for helping me through the madness which is the A to Z – especially bang in the middle of a house move!

Acknowledgement

Introduction

THE SCOTTISH SUN'S A to Z feature is synonymous with the SuperGoals pull-out every Monday during the football season. It's not your typical footballer's interview but more of an insight into the depraved dressing rooms of our game. And then some!

Players are always desperate to find out their ratings on a Monday – but they also check to see if they are mentioned in the infamous A to Z. And they are wonderfully portrayed by Scotland's top cartoonist Malky McCormick.

It's a place where the stars get to dish the dirt on their teammates and slag them rotten. It can make or break their Monday. It's full of insults, secrets, lurid tales, boozy benders, debauchery and the most elaborate of pranks. Nothing is out of bounds and some have even been toned down for a family newspaper. Then there are just the plain silly moments which will have a player in tears from laughter. It is a break from the seriousness of football and reminds us that football is just a funny old game.

The A to Z started out in 1997 when journalists such as Gary Ralston, Gary Keown, Chris Gilmour and Ewan Smith contributed. It grew to be a real favourite and has been continued over the years by Iain King, Robert Grieve, Gareth Law, Paul Hughes, Roger Hannah and myself. I assumed the mantle as main A to Zer in the 2001/2002 season and have racked up over 300 of them since.

Every Christmas, we compile a 'best A to Z of the year' and it always throws a challenge – so many good stories but so little space. I'd find myself with over fifty cracking stories and having to whittle it down. That got me thinking about compiling a book. If I was picking fifty great stories a year then surely thirteen years worth would fill a book.

The book moved quickly. A green light from the editor David Dinsmore and head of Sport Iain King kicked it off. The painstaking bit was going through almost 500 A to Zs which frazzled the brain. I picked 110,000 words and had another tough task of cutting it down to 60,000 then sorting them into chapters. It was a long process but it was also a laugh-a-minute. I hope you enjoy reading it as much as I enjoyed compiling it.

Arf Arf

THERE is nothing like a good old belly laugh! Here are some tales which had our players creasing with laughter whether it was boys being boys, daft comments or some comedy timing. This is a selection of comedy gold moments.

COLIN CRAMB (Football journeyman): I was following Paul McGrillen and John Paul McBride in a car from Stirling after training, when they spotted two hitch-hikers with a sign for Glasgow. They stopped about 100 yards ahead and JP shouted on them to hop in. The two hitch-hikers chucked their sign in the bushes and started to carry their rucksacks. But just as they got to the car, Mowgli and JP drove off. It was absolutely priceless.

GREG SHIELDS (Dunfermline ginger): Scott Thomson was talking about how he had the largest **** in Fife – and whipped it out on the table tennis table to show everyone. What he didn't realise was that there was a work experience girl, who was only about sixteen, standing behind him. Every time she saw him after that, she kept showing him her pinkie.

KENNY DEUCHAR (Dr Goals): We had our own kangaroo court at Falkirk. If a player was accused of something and it made it to the court, there was a 99.9 per cent chance you'd be found guilty, even if you were in fact innocent. Well, Steven Rennie was found guilty – he was innocent – but he had to do the forfeit because the majority rules. He had to strip naked except for the daily donkey jumper, which was tiny, and walk the groundsman's dog round the outside of the Brockville pitch with everyone cheering and shouting abuse. The dog stopped a few times to take a pee and even once for a number two. It was hilarious.

WARREN HAWKE (Sunderland, Morton, Queen of the South): I was at Sunderland playing in a derby game against Newcastle at St James' Park. Our manager then was Terry Butcher and he came into the changing room with a No.1 haircut all over. He claimed we were paratroopers and said that our mission was to storm in, nick the three points and escape as fast as we could. You should have seen the players' faces – they were a picture. Unfortunately, the mission was a failure as we lost.

STEVE PATERSON (Caley Thistle legend): I became mates with Tommy Docherty when I played for him in Sydney in 1983. Every day was a laugh. I won $500 for five numbers in the lottery and bought a pink Volkswagen Beetle. I picked the Doc up for training and he'd wear a Frankenstein mask and stick his head out the window to frighten people. He also used to lie on the conveyor belt at the baggage reclaim and go round half a dozen times. It was hilarious.

JOHN HUGHES (Falkirk, Hibs): My favourite ground is Tynecastle. I remember one Hearts fan giving me pelters while I was warming up in front of him. He kept going on at me, but he had the biggest ginger barnet. Eventually I turned round and said: "Big yin, if I had a big ginger barnet like that, I'd be wearing a balaclava." All his mates were laughing. He sat down after that.

DON HUTCHISON (Scotland legend): There was a fight between Phil Thompson and a YTS boy at Liverpool. They had a square-up and Phil told him to get his medals on the table. But the young boy said to Phil: "Get your toes on the table." Phil only has nine! We were all crying on the floor.

MARC TWADDLE (Falkirk, Partick Thistle): Falkirk were playing Rangers at Ibrox and John Hughes was giving his team-talk in the dressing room. There was a big white board and he got a marker pen and started to write on it. He wrote QUIESTIONS on the board. We could see he hadn't spelt it correctly and were all sniggering. Vitor Lima – who hardly spoke any English – walked up, licked his thumb and rubbed out the I. Yogi realised what he had done and just started laughing.

CHRIS SWAILES (Ipswich Town, Rotherham, Hamilton): I played with Steve Sedgley at Ipswich and he could fart any time he wanted. I remember one time in the dressing room he was completely naked, went down on all fours, cocked his leg like a dog and played a tune.

EAMONN BANNON (Dundee United, Hearts): Mark Walters had just signed for Rangers and Hugh Burns, then at Hearts, was getting wound up about marking him by gaffer Alex McDonald. Hugh was so worked up in the tunnel he asked which one was Mark! He had to be told he was the only black player in Scotland at that time.

GERRY COLLINS (Partick Thistle): I do like dressing up for fancy dress parties. When we had an annual Dukla Pumpherston dinner, I dressed up as the Pope. We were introduced to the top table singing 'The Sash' in Latin, which was funny.

IAN WILSON (Leicester City, Everton, Peterhead): I used to get a lot of stick when I played with Everton because my hair was receding and I remember getting a lot of abuse from Liverpool fans in a derby game. I went to take a throw in but then suddenly a wig landed right next to me, so I put it on and took the throw-in.

ANDY MCLAREN (Dundee United and wide boy of Scottish football): I was playing golf with Henrik Larsson when he shot a hole-in-one at Tom Boyd's golf outing. That was at the time when he had scored 100 goals for Celtic and he could do no wrong. Andy Cameron was playing in front of us and when the ball went in, he suggested to Henrik he should also walk across the pond next to it!

JIM DUFFY (Baldy coot of a manager): I met Daryl Hannah in a bar in London but I was more dumbstruck than starstruck. My mate Stuart Rafferty was at the other end of the bar and I was trying desperately to let him know who was standing right beside me without making it obvious it was a big deal. But Raff clocked who it was and pointed across while shouting at the top of his voice: "F***, it's Daryl Hannah, by the way!"

JACK ROSS (Clyde, Falkirk, St Mirren and media darling): Brian Carrigan won the Second Division Player of the Year award and was plastered when he arrived. He somehow managed to get himself sorted when he went to pick up his prize but then spoiled it by doing a Chick Young impersonation – when Chick was giving him his award!

JIMMY NICHOLL (Northern Ireland, Manchester United, Rangers, Raith Rovers): One day in our hotel in Mexico, a three-foot iguana walked into reception and we jumped out of our skins. The security guard said it was harmless, picked it up and put it in a box. Later on, Billy Hamilton and I invited the rest of the squad to our room for a game of cards. The match was heating up as I left the room to get the iguana and wrapped it in a towel before throwing it on to the middle of the table. You've never seen grown men run so fast.

OWEN COYLE (Top player and top manager): Andy Walker has the most amazing way of eating cream cakes. He licks all the cream perfectly from the cake then eats the middle – it takes him about twenty minutes. One day at Bolton, we were celebrating Alan Thompson's birthday with cream cakes and the lads decided to fill the middle of Andy's with a bar of soap. We all sat there waiting for THE moment. The cream went, then suddenly Andy's face turned sour as he bit into the soap.

NICK COLGAN (Irish keeper at Hibs for five years): I played for the Chelsea youth team with a lad called Terry Skiverton and what a character he was. In one game, he scored a superb goal and to celebrate he chased after the referee, jumped on his back and demanded a piggyback ride. Everyone was in stitches apart from the referee who booked him.

CHRIS MCGROARTY (Dunfermline): I'll never forget Johnston Bellshaw for one comedy moment. I played with him in the Highland League for Ross County and one day at Fort William, he came into his own. He was subbed late on and because he was so short-sighted he sat in the wrong dugout. He sat there hurling abuse at what he thought was our manager. The guy turned to him and said: "Listen laddie, I'm not your boss." We were laughing so much on the pitch the ref stopped the game until the fuss died down.

BILLY MCNEILL (Lisbon Lion): Bobby Lennox had unbelievably long arms, he was like an orangutan and he hated being mocked about it. We checked into an airport one day and there was an advertising campaign for something with massive posters of apes all over the place. We didn't have to say anything. He kept saying: "I see the pictures, just f*****g shut up!"

TAM MACDONALD (Scottish Junior legend): Willie Thompson at Talbot, who went on to Airdrie, was one of those wee, stocky right-wingers you get in our game. At one game a punter shouted: "Haw, did yer maw conceive when the circus was in town ya **** ye!" Killer line. The only time I ever saw that boy speechless.

ROBERT SNODGRASS (Livingston, Leeds United): Graham Dorrans, Lee Matthews and I phoned up one of those chat-lines. I said my girlfriend and I used to stay on a farm and when we'd make love I'd hear farm noises. I told her that I wanted her to do the same so I had this woman on the other end of the phone making pig noises and cow noises then she even kidded on that she was a duck.

RAY FARNINGHAM (Forfar Athletic, Dundee): Neil McCann and James Grady were up to no good in the hotel when we were in Bournemouth with Dundee on pre-season so Gerry Britton and I decided to get them back. We went to the local pet store and tried to buy a snake or a rat but they didn't have any so we got two gerbils instead and put them in their room. They complained constantly about scratching noises for three or four days.

TOMMY BURNS (Celtic legend – R.I.P.): John Doyle was with the Scotland squad and one of the boys phoned him up pretending to be a scout from an English club. They arranged a meeting at the pub round the corner from the hotel but John never told anyone about it and sneaked off to the pub. He was sitting, waiting in the corner when the lads walked in and burst out laughing at him. I think Gordon McQueen and Asa Hartford were involved in that one.

ASA HARTFORD (Scotland Hall of Famer): Mick Summerbee was at Manchester City when we played Everton at Goodison. There was a break in the game and Mick was leaning against the corner flag. The Everton fans started chanting "Pinocchio, Pinocchio" because he'd a huge blower. Mick turned round to look at them and then blew his nose using the corner flag.

TOM STEVEN (ex-Cowdenbeath boss): The ball was kicked out by the keeper in a reserve game between Hibs and Partick when Johnny Hamilton pulled the bottom of his top out and let the ball bounce underneath his jersey. He ran about with the ball stuck up it, pretending he never knew where it was. The referee didn't have a clue where the ball had gone and everyone was in hysterics.

MARVYN WILSON (Airdrie, Ayr, Hamilton, Clyde): Stephen Docherty got drunk really quickly and started doing a Funky Chicken dance. After about half an hour, he started showing our boss Sandy Stewart how to do a slide tackle in the nightclub – let's just say Sandy wished he'd put some shin guards on.

MARTIN GLANCY (Stirling Albion, Airdrie): Willie Wilson broke a piece of soap in half and placed the pieces in with the biscuits in the Airdrie players' lounge. Our kit-man JD, John Donnelly, picked a bit up and ate it. It was hilarious because he was spitting soap everywhere.

DAVIE IRONS (ex-Gretna and Morton manager): Rowan Alexander and Brookes Mileson had a local reporter convinced we were signing Henrik Larsson in the summer because everyone was going on about us being millionaires. The paper had the back page ready and was about to go to press with the story before the truth came out. We had a team photo with Larsson superimposed in the back row.

JERRY O'DRISCOLL (Dundee): We had just won the First Division when we received our medals but Dave Rodgers was down in England getting treatment. So Jim McInally decided to buy a cheap £1.99 medal and got –Div 1– engraved on it. He gave it to Dave who moaned that he'd grafted all season to get a piece of crap like that. We kept it up for a week.

PAUL MCGRILLEN (Motherwell, Falkirk – R.I.P.): We had a night off with Partick in Blackpool and went back to the B&B at about 3am. John Lambie was at the bar hammering the drinks back and Allan Moore waved a £50 note at him and asked if he'd seen one before. John just took it off him and bought everyone doubles. Poor Allan got about £4 change back. The next morning he asked John about getting the money back because it was to last him for four days but John looked at him and told him to get lost.

FRANK MCAVENNIE (Playboy): St Mirren were in Rotterdam playing Feyenoord in the UEFA Cup when Frank McDougall was sent off. As he walked off, he was shouting and swearing at the officials and fans – but walked down the wrong tunnel. He waited ten minutes, thinking no one would notice, but he got dog's abuse trying to sneak back. I had tears streaming down my face.

GRAHAM BAYNE (Dundee, Caley Thistle, Dunfermline): The funniest thing I've seen is Darren Dods trying to do the Johan Cruyff turn in training. He isn't the most graceful of players, which is why he used it just in training. I once burnt my fingers when I decided to clean the cooker but I forgot it was still hot and got painful blisters.

BRYAN PRUNTY (Aberdeen, Caley Thistle, Airdrie): Celtic's youth team were playing Hearts in Musselburgh. Mark Fotheringham had been sent off and Tommy Burns wasn't happy. After the game, Tommy picked up the nearest training bag and threw it down. He didn't realise there was a ghetto blaster in the bag and he smashed it to pieces. Everyone was desperately trying to hold their laughter in because he was very angry.

MARK MCGHEE (Aberdeen legend): I was driving with Tam Burns and George McCluskey down Maryhill Road when we spotted someone going into an off-licence. We were talking about how the girl with the curly hair had a wonderful a**e. But when she turned around, it was actually Davie Provan in his platforms and flares. We were mortified.

LIAM BUCHANAN (Partick Thistle hitman): We were getting thumped by Gretna in a Third Division game – it was 6-0 at half time. Gary Fusco suddenly said: "Let's try and keep this below 10!"

At the time we weren't laughing, but looking back, it was hilarious. In the end we lost 8-0, which was embarrassing enough.

JOHN MACDONALD (Rangers hero): Hugh Burns was chucking water over Ally McCoist one day, so Ally got Hugh's suit jacket, went into the showers and then everyone else started chucking water over him, which is what Ally wanted, to ruin Hugh's jacket.

ARTHUR NUMAN (Rangers Dutch legend): At PSV, every player got a red Opel from the sponsor. Someone switched all the keys so we couldn't open our cars. You could only open the car by putting the key in the door. It took some of us two hours to find our cars.

DAVID PROCTOR (Airdrie, Dundee United, Caley Thistle): At Inverness, we were staying in a hotel in Brora when I phoned up Juanjo and Richard Hastings pretending to be the hotel receptionist. I asked them what newspapers they wanted in the morning. Next morning, they came down raging and moaning how the papers didn't arrive.

ANDY TOD (Dunfermline): Gerry Britton was brilliant. I remember one game at East End Park, which he wasn't playing in. He stole the microphone that the Tannoy announcer used. During the second half, he used it to read out Bert Paton's car registration, asking the owner to return to his vehicle. He'd also start shouting: "If you're happy and you know it clap your hands!"

GEORGE MCCLUSKEY (Celtic hero): One day, Davie Provan put on Johnny Doyle's trousers. Johnny shoved Davie into the bath not realising he had his own trousers on.

PAUL MCHALE (Clyde, Dundee): There were five minutes left of our Scottish Cup win over Celtic in 2006 when Joe Miller decided to come on while we were 2-1 up so he could play against his old team. After about twenty seconds, he gave chase down the line but tripped and smashed his face on the ball. I was injured for the game but was in the stand and couldn't stop laughing.

WILLIE MILLER (Aberdeen legend and Scotland Hall of Famer): We were playing in Romania when Fergie smashed some teacups and then gave an old fashioned tea-urn a forearm smash. But it didn't budge an inch. He grimaced in pain while I tried to stifle my laughter. His face went pale but he continued talking although we knew he wanted to scream in pain.

JIM PATERSON (Dundee United, Motherwell): I was with the Scotland Under-21s when we played away in Bosnia. Gary Naysmith went to take a long throw but as he walked back he disappeared – he fell down a drain that had its cover off. He got stuck and had to be helped out.

CLAYTON DONALDSON (Hibs): At York City, there was a guy called James Dudgeon and he stuck some heat rub into Lewis McMahon's hair gel. All the lads were waiting for him to come out the shower and within five seconds of using this stuff his head started to burn and go red. It was funny watching him run back into the showers to try and wash it out.

ALAN MCINALLY (Good friend of Klaus Augenthaler in Bayern in Munich): Ally McCoist must be the only player I know that could get a telephone number from a girl during a game, and not just any game. At the Italia '90 World Cup, we were on the bench yet he still managed to chat up an Italian girl. She was a darling. How could she want him instead of me?

MIKE FRASER (Caley Thistle and Motherwell keeper): At Caley, the apprentices used to go outside the stadium and play a game of touch where you would try and keep the ball in the air. Gary McGowan booted the ball square in Mark Brown's face and he was raging. As he was one of the senior players, we were all trying not to laugh, but Mark was so angry he booted the minibus and left a dent in it.

RYAN MCCANN (Scored a goal from eighty-four yards for Queen of the South): The Hartlepool players were in Magaluf and we were sitting in this bar when we broke a chair, but didn't make it obvious. We sat there the whole day and watched about twenty people in total sit on the chair and fall over, soaking themselves with drink. The best bit though was when the manager Neale Cooper sat down in the chair and spilled his pint over himself.

ROBBIE RAESIDE (Dundee, Peterhead): When Dougie Cameron, Ryan Blackadder and Kevin Fotheringham stood in the East Fife wall, they looked like Right Said Fred.

SIMON LYNCH: (Celtic, Dundee, Airdrie) At Ronnie Moran's testimonial game at Anfield, I was sitting next to Jonathan Gould on the bench. On the seat next to him was a microphone that was linked up to the stadium's Tannoy system. Gouldy spent the game starting up Celtic songs for the travelling support and no one ever knew it was him.

GERRY MCCABE (Clydebank, Dumbarton): I was with Cork City in 1991 when we played Bayern Munich in the UEFA Cup. We lost 2-0 over there, 3-1 on aggregate. The boys wanted their strips after the game and we all piled into the dressing room at the Olympic Stadium to raid their hamper. We grabbed shirts, jock straps, socks, you name it. Their manager Jupp Heynckes was getting stuck right into his players – but we just barged in. The room fell into silence as we dipped into everything. I got Thomas Berthold's shirt.

DAVID RAE (Charismatic Queen of the South chairman): When Roy Henderson played in goals for Queens in the late '40s, early '50s, he was quite a ladies' man. One time he was chatting to a couple of girls behind his goal and the next thing the ball flew into the back of the net.

MARC TWADDLE: Falkirk were playing Livi when Paddy Cregg and Stephen O'Donnell were trying to wind up Paul Lambert, who was playing. They were saying he was past it and how his legs had gone. Paul just said: "It's all the money in my pocket that is slowing me down." That shut them up.

CHRIS JARDINE (Annan Athletic): Grant Parker made himself an ice ball when it was snowing and threw it at our old assistant manager Kevin Robison. It missed him by millimetres but if it had hit him it would have killed him. Kevin was absolutely raging and was chasing Grant around saying he was going to punch his lights out.

GARY MCDONALD (Kilmarnock, Aberdeen): Some of the Aberdeen boys got the key to Sandy Clark's room, bought about 300 balloons, blew them up and stuffed them in his room. Sandy couldn't get in. It took a lot of dedication but it won't take a genius to work out who did it.

JOHN MCMASTER (Aberdeen, Morton): Morton were playing Raith Rovers at Stark's Park and Allan McGraw was raging when we lost the ball. He threw his walking sticks on to the pitch in a rage but of course he needed them for his bad knees and could hardly stand.

KEVIN MCDONALD (Airdrie): We had a Christmas night out with Airdrie. We were all sitting having a Chinese meal as we had been out all day with a few of the lads a bit worse for wear. We turned around to see Marc Smyth with his socks and shoes off trying to catch fish in the pond. Luckily he didn't get spotted by the staff.

BRIAN MARTIN (Falkirk, St Mirren, Motherwell stopper): Tam Forsyth took training at Strathclyde Park but while we were stretching, this big swan came out of the pond and started following him. He was trying to shoo the swan away, which was hilarious. And to top that, Tam said: "That's the biggest goose I've ever seen."

DAVID PROCTOR: We were on a team building day out at RAF Lossiemouth in pre-season and visited the dog section. They asked if anyone wanted to put on the protective body suit to demonstrate how a dog would attack an intruder. Our coach Scott Kellacher volunteered and he ended up being dragged along the ground by the biggest and most vicious dog you've seen.

Bad Habits

WIND, picking noses or pongy feet – which of your footballing idols has annoying traits which get on their team-mates wick?

ALEX WILLIAMS (Clyde, Morton, Playboy, Wideboy): Stevie Masterton acts like a woman. At Clyde, we would call him Charlene. He phoned his sister one time while we were driving and asked her if she could do his hair that night. He has curly hair but uses hair tongs to straighten it.

ROBBIE RAESIDE: I have terrible wind. When John McGlashan was giving his team-talk, I would be the only one brave enough to break a few raspers – he just looked at me and shook his head.

ZANDER DIAMOND (Aberdeen): My worst habit used to be dating psycho birds from Aberdeen. They are all totally off their heads. I advise anyone not to go near them because they are rockets. You got the groupies who would hang around you and once you snogged them, they want to end up being your wife. My advice would be not to date an ex's best pal. I'm probably going to get chased out of Aberdeen for this.

ALLY MACMILLAN (Elgin City): I experienced road rage when an OAP had her indicator on for a left turn but she was talking to her pal and not looking at the road so she ended up driving over to the right. When we pulled up at the lights, I put my window down just to give her what for and there she was, bold as brass, sticking her fingers up at me. I just laughed and put the window up. You just could not buy that.

JOHN POTTER (Dunfermline, Clyde, St Mirren defender): I can wear underwear for two or three days in a row. If I am in a rush and I see them lying on the floor, I'll turn them inside out and stick them on. I don't like shaving either and sometimes I look a right tink when I come to training.

JOHN MCVEIGH (Ex-Partick, Raith, Stenhousemuir, Albion Rovers boss): Graham Hay had every excuse in the book when he couldn't make training. He came up with tales of his mum's house being on fire, his auntie's house was burgled, his car was set on fire – he was unbelievable and we used to call him 'The Dodge Book'. The most bizarre one was when I was a coach at Falkirk, a young boy called Roland Fabiani was an hour late. He said a lorry load of fish emptied over his car while he was at the lights. I didn't believe him but sure enough the next day there was a picture of his car in the paper . . . covered in fish.

JOHN HILLCOAT (Goalie of many clubs): I pick my toenails. I don't know why I do it. I leave them all over the floor. George O'Boyle used to drive me nuts when I shared a room with him. He used to grind his teeth in his sleep.

LEE WILKIE (Dundee, Dundee United prankster): I have a tendency to pick my nostril hairs. I don't know why I do it. I am always checking for hairs and I will either use my fingers or tweezers. It makes my eyes water though.

STUART TAYLOR (St Mirren, Falkirk, Airdrie, Hamilton): Paul Armstrong would fart all the time and it was really smelly. He used to play tunes under his covers. He is the only person I know who can play a high C note with his bum cheeks. I had to leave the windows open.

SCOTT MURRAY (Bristol City): I have a few bad habits – I am always biting my nails and have done since I was a kid. I also tend to pick the hairs out of my nose and my eyebrows.

BARRY ROBSON (Caley Thistle, Dundee United, Celtic, Middlesbrough, Scotland): I stayed in digs with Scott McLean for two years and his hygiene wasn't great. One time, when we had showered and were getting ready to go out, he didn't have any clean underwear. He raked through the dirty laundry basket and got a pair of training shorts, which had dirt marks on them, and wore them to go out.

CHRIS MCGROARTY: I would let off in the car on the way to training when I travelled with Owen Coyle and a few other lads. Every time they smelled something funny, I blamed the car heater.

RAY FARNINGHAM: Davie Irons had the worst pong from his feet, which was terrible. They were really smelly and he used to cut his toenails in the room too.

PAUL DEVLIN (Birmingham City, Scotland): I pick my scabs. If I have one, I can never leave it alone. I am also a fidgeter because I get bored quite easily so maybe that is why I do it. During pre-season, if I get grass burns, I will end up picking at my scab and have blood seeping from it.

JOHN PAUL MCBRIDE (St Johnstone, Partick Thistle): I fart a lot and also bite my nails.

STEVE BOWEY (Queen of the South Geordie): I flick through the TV channels, I fart a lot and I spit while I'm driving.

DEREK TOWNSLEY (Motherwell, Hibs, Gretna): The less said about sharing a room with Davie Nicholls, the better. Everyone who has shared with Davie will know what I mean. You have to sleep with one eye open. He does have some very strange dreams.

WILLIE KINNIBURGH (Motherwell, Partick Thistle): My worst habit is swearing around the house, particularly around

Rian, which is terrible. I'm f*****g murder at doing that. I forget he's around. Liam Buchanan sits in the dressing room with his legs at ten to two and shaves every hair on his body. And Kevin McKinlay helps him with the bits he can't reach. I don't need to tell you where that is.

RYAN MCGUFFIE (Gretna): Derek Townsley would fold his Y-fronts then put them on top of his trainers in the dressing room, which drove me mad. I have put shampoo in his underwear to get him to stop doing it but he didn't take the hint.

TREVOR MOLLOY (Motherwell): Paul Keegan would brush his teeth before he goes onto the pitch and no one knew why because it is an unusual thing to do. I think it is maybe a superstition.

DYLAN KERR (Kilmarnock Scottish Cup winner): My worst habit was peeing into the drinks of people I didn't like.

CHRIS KILLEN (Hibs, Celtic, New Zealand): I need to aim better when I go the toilet. Hannah always wants the seat down so I just leave it.

BILLY MEHMET (St Mirren): The bravest thing I ever did was sit next to Eddie Malone in a car with his bad breath. I got into his car after training one day and noticed it straight away.

GARY ARBUCKLE (Clyde): If you were sitting reading a newspaper, Michael McGowan would have this annoying habit of coming up to you and karate chopping it out of your hands. It was funny the first few times but got boring.

CRAIG SAMSON (Ginger ex-Scotland Under-21 star): Derek Lyle has a bit of a strange fetish for talking about his own private parts. Once when I walked into Ross County's dressing room, Martin 'Jimmy' Scott was shaving his legs. I have no idea why he was doing it but there were some strange things going on in that dressing room.

ALEX KEDDIE (Ross County): Sean Higgins would shave his private parts – front and back. And what made it worse was he did it in front of all the boys. Some of the positions he gets into are quite frightening.

BRIAN WAKE (Morton striker with a perm): I felt sorry for my old room-mate at Morton, Ryan McGuffie. We went down to Newcastle for a few days and the beds were a bit too close for comfort. He was rudely awoken by me putting my arm around him in the wee dark hours of the morning. He says he slept with his a**e against the wall the rest of that night!

WILLIE MILLER: Doug Rougvie would take his falsers out and put them in his pocket before a game.

DANNY GRAINGER (Dundee United, St Johnstone): Sean Dillon is very strange. If you bang into his elbow you have to tap his other elbow ten times. He is a bit OCD and a bit of a weirdo. Everything has to be folded perfectly on his bench too.

DANNY CADAMARTERI (Everton, Dundee United): Since coming to Dundee United, I think I have tried to bond quite well with my new team-mates. However, I am becoming increasingly concerned with one of my team-mates in particular, who seems to be obsessed with my body and, without fail, manages to comment on it every single day. I took it as a compliment at first, but I am now beginning to think he wants to be a little bit more than my team-mate. He knows who he is.

Boozy Antics

FOOTBALLERS treat their bodies like temples during the season – but when it comes to a night out after a game, boy do they go nuts. They can't handle their drink and here are the reasons why . . .

MARK ROBERTS (Airdrie, Partick, Kilmarnock): I once threw myself down some stairs to get myself some attention. I was on the karaoke singing Bon Jovi's 'Living on a Prayer' but no one was taking any notice of me on the stage because I think they were embarrassed by me. I had been drinking a lot so I just decided I'd throw myself down some stairs. Luckily I didn't injure myself. It was pretty stupid and I think it made the audience even more embarrassed for me.

CHRIS MILLAR (Morton, St Johnstone): Morton players trashed a hotel in Banff on pre-season. We had a few drinks on the last night and ended up in one of the rooms. We were jumping on the bed, things were getting broken and bottles were flying. We climbed on to a roof outside and people suggested we all stripped. John Maisano was wearing red pants, which we grabbed from him and burned. Next morning it turned out we caused £700 worth of damage, but we all chipped in.

JIM LAUCHLAN (Kilmarnock, Dundee United, Dundee): I played with Stevie Thompson for Scotland Under-21s and at Dundee United. His party piece was to either bite your neck or, if you were sitting on a chair, he would start benchpressing the chair. He would drink the vinegar in Da Vinci's as well. When Marko Roberts was at a certain stage with a pint, he'd pour it over his head.

ROBBIE RAESIDE: We had a great Christmas night at Raith Rovers – there was Elvis, Darth Vader, the Three Musketeers and Tarzan running amok in Kirkcaldy High Street. The chief inspector brought the CCTV footage the next day for Jimmy Nicholl to see – but luckily he was a Raith fan!

ADAM COAKLEY (Motherwell, Queen's Park): Michael Gardyne, Dean Keenan and I were in Royal Exchange Square in Glasgow on a drinking session when Michael climbed up on the Duke of Wellington statue and peed from the top of the horse. I couldn't move for laughing.

DYLAN KERR: I was a massive fan of Gary Glitter. But on the very same day he got caught for being a pervert, I was actually dressed up as him on a night out in the Horseshoe Bar in Glasgow.

I was taking a leak when the guy next to me spat at me. I had no idea why as I hadn't seen the news that day. I said: "What was that for?" and he just said: "You f***** sick pervert b******!" I ended up going to a second-hand shop to buy a leather glove and plastic emerald ring. When anyone asked, I said I was Alvin Stardust.

JIMMY THOMSON (ex-Dunfermline, Berwick, Alloa, Raith boss): Frank McGarvey and Keith Knox ran a card school at Clyde and promised punishment for whoever fell asleep first. Well, I was blitzed, wasn't I? And I dozed off. And when I woke up they'd shaved off my eyebrows, the top half of my sides and Knox had tried to shave my head before being dragged off. I missed the team photo.

SIMON MENSING (Hamilton midfielder): The St Johnstone lads had their Christmas night out in Liverpool. We were in this night club and Neil Janczyk was challenged to a dance by a sixty-year-old woman. Neil, being the guy he is, obliged and it was like the scene in *American Pie: The Wedding*. It was some sight when she went through his legs. They both got an ovation at the end.

CHRIS HILLCOAT (Hamilton): Paul McDonald was on holiday one year and as per usual we went daft with the drink. For some reason he got it into his head he could turn the tables over. The police came and tried to arrest him. As they came to get him Paul just stepped back and said: "Your faces are noted." It was hilarious. They shoved him in the clink to sober up and let him out in the morning.

SCOTT MURRAY: I was at the PFA awards in London when I smashed my false teeth. I had won best right winger in the league and when I got up I fell over because I was so p****d. I don't remember much about it. At an awards do the year before, we stayed in a hotel and thought we would large it up in London. We lost one of the lads, Lee Matthews, but we found him sitting in bins outside a club in his hired tuxedo. We took him back to sober him up and put him in the shower but he fell asleep in the bath.

CRAIG MCKEOWN (Clyde, Dundee): Paul McHale's wedding, which was a three-day event in Stirling a few summers ago, was very funny. The wedding party were in the foyer when Stevie Masterton walked in and made reference to what his 'Mini Mastie' – pointing to his privates – was going to get up to with a stunning girl he had pulled. The place was in total hysterics.

LEE MAIR (Dundee, Dundee United, Aberdeen, St Mirren): Jamie Langfield and I both stayed over at Gavin Rae's place, and Jamie had to go back early because he was so drunk. When Gavin and I came back later on, we noticed that the top of the stairs was soaking. We knew Jamie had been so drunk he had peed there, but in the morning, when he obviously realised what he had done, he tried to cover it up, put an empty cup beside it and said he had spilled a cup of tea. Gavin and I were in stitches and Jamie still denies it to this day.

BILLY KIRKWOOD (Dundee United legend): We were flying back from a European game with Dundee United and were allowed a few beers on the plane. But I got hauled in to see Jim McLean the next day – he fined me £25 because he thought I was enjoying myself too much.

GAVIN RAE (Dundee, Rangers, Cardiff City): I went on a night out in Glasgow with my two best mates in football – Dennis Wyness and Jamie Watt. We stayed in the same room in a hotel and for some reason Dennis thought it would be funny if he took his belt out quickly and whacked me in the arm. I felt pain but when I woke up there was blood all over my bed and I knew it was bad. I had to get the physio at Dundee to sort it out and I don't think he was too chuffed.

BARRY MCLAUGHLIN (Former St Mirren captain): I was so drunk when I turned eighteen that the bouncer wouldn't let me into a nightclub. I had to go to McDonald's to try and sober up. Next thing I knew, I was chatting up some seventy-year-old lady, that's all I remember until the morning. Then I woke up and saw some hairy a**e and wondered what I had done. It turned out I had crashed out at my mate Johnny Matrecano's place – thank God.

STEVIE TOSH (Fifer with a big gob): We had a golf day out when I was at St Johnstone and there was loads of free drink. Needless to say a few of us got drunk and fell asleep on someone's floor. Kevin McGowne, Allan Preston, Iain Ferguson and Roddy

Grant were all there and we had a right laugh. Then I woke up to find Roddy had shaved most of my hair off. I had a few patches left and had to go to the barber's to get my whole head shaved. I had to wear a silly hat for the next few weeks and the Saints fans were chanting "Vialli" at me.

SCOTT WALKER (St Mirren, Brechin): I was my brother Mark's best man and supposed to be staying sober at his stag do so I could look after him. But I ended up getting so drunk that I collapsed into my bed. When I woke up the next day, there was vomit everywhere – and I had missed my brother's wedding suit by three inches. I felt so bad about it but we didn't have time to argue and he cleaned the mess up before we rushed to the wedding.

MIKE TEASDALE (Caley Thistle legend): On my stag night, I was completely drunk after my pals bought me two cocktail pints. One cost £25 and the other £18. Luckily my wife was also on her hen night miles away from us because I was so drunk I had to be carried out of the nightclub and put in a taxi. Next morning I woke up, looked around the room and didn't have a clue where I was, then I saw blonde hair next to me and wondered what I had done. Thank God when I raised the covers, it was my wife.

CHRIS INNES (Kilmarnock, Gretna, Dundee United, St Mirren): I'd gone to Tony Bullock's fancy dress party with the missus in Dundee and locked myself out the house. I was blootered but had to clamber up a drainpipe on to the window ledge on the second floor dressed as Fred Flintstone.

STEVE LOVELL (Dundee, Aberdeen): During one summer, all the Dundee lads went out for the day. I wasn't planning to drink but ended up wrecked. I was a disgrace. I only know Lee Wilkie took me home in a taxi because he told me so – I can't remember anything that happened. I woke up the next day, lying on the bathroom floor and covered in vomit. There was also mud on the carpet between the front door and where I was lying. Big Lee reckons that's because I fell into the flowerbeds when he poured me out the taxi.

KEVIN KYLE (Mouthy Scotland and Hearts striker): I keep in touch with all the boys in Stranraer I worked with on the Stena Line and we go over to a place just outside Larne for a barbecue and a few beers. Years ago, we set off at 9.30am and I had my first pint at 10am. We got the slow boat back to Stranraer at 9pm, which gets you back in at 1.30am. By that point I'd had seventeen pints and my mate had twenty-seven. When we arrived back we went to a nightclub for the last fifteen minutes before going for a naked swim in the local marina at 3am.

RICKY GILLIES (St Mirren, Aberdeen): There was one time a few years ago when I was out on the town with Jim Lauchlan. We'd had a few and went down a little lane to do the toilet but while we were standing against the wall a police van came round the corner. Jim stopped what he was doing and just started walking away and the police came over and lifted me. The van drove off but when we got alongside Jim, it stopped and he was told to get in beside me. I suppose it isn't something we should be proud of but it was quite funny. The coppers just told us we were out of order and we apologised. Thankfully that was the end of it.

STEVE CONVERY (Clyde, Hamilton): I was once lifted by the police when I was eighteen for singing. I was on a night out with friends when we were on our way home and I was singing in the street. The police told me to stop but I kept at it and they arrested me. I was put in the cells overnight and charged with breach of the peace. I was fined £100, which I thought was harsh.

SCOTT MCLEAN (Professional daftie and world record holder for A to Z mentions): After a game at Caley, Martin Glancy, Stuart Golabek and I decided to hop on a train when we didn't know where it was taking us. We weren't due back to training until Tuesday morning at 10am so we ended up in Newcastle. We stayed there until 2am on Tuesday morning and had to get a taxi to Glasgow which cost a fortune and then the train to Inverness. We made it in time for training, although we were still the worse for wear.

ALLAN PRESTON (Dundee United, Hearts, St Johnstone): We were at a nightclub in Inverness when Roddy Grant bet he could whip down this girl's ski pants before she could grab hold of them. Gary Bollan, Paul Kane and Alan Kernaghan were there and we put money on the bar. Roddy went over and whipped her ski pants down – but she wasn't wearing anything underneath. We grabbed our money back while the girl turned round and thumped Kieran McAnespie because she thought he'd done it.

ALAN MAYBURY (Hearts, Leeds United): I have seen Gary Kelly do a headstand in a bin on a night out. We just turned around and there he was in one of these grey bins.

COLIN MCMENAMIN (Livingston, Gretna, Dundee hotshot): I was in a pub in Dumfries with friends when we stole all the balls from the pool table. It must have been the drink – it seemed like good fun at the time.

GRAHAM ROBERTS (Tottenham, Rangers, England): After a game against Motherwell, I parked my car on the steps of the hotel I was staying in. The hotel asked me to move it the next morning but I don't remember it getting there. Had I been drinking? No comment.

COLIN CRAMB: I was with Gary O'Connor at Doncaster. We ended up going out from the Saturday to the Thursday. When we eventually got home, Gary stuck me in an Asda trolley and pushed me the two miles home through the main street. The next morning I woke up and the trolley was in the front garden along with a traffic cone.

STEVIE MILNE (Dundee, St Johnstone): All the lads from Dundee, like Gavin Rae and Lee Wilkie, came out for my twenty-first birthday. All I can remember is throwing up in the toilet at the Mardi Gras nightclub, getting thrown out, meeting Leeanne outside, and then being sick again in the taxi home. They were buying me pints of everything that night, especially Gavin.

COLIN STEWART (Goalie, son of Scotland and Rangers keeper Jim): I was with the Scotland Under-21s over in Poland and we'd been having a few drinks. Kevin Kyle passed out so Jamie Langfield decided to use a fire extinguisher to wake him up. But it was one of those chalk ones that doesn't stop until it is empty. The room was totally white and everyone was covered in the stuff. We were flying home the next morning and Kevin and Mark Burchill had their suits covered in chalk.

ANDY DOWIE (Rangers, Partick, Ross County, Dunfermline): I slipped on a night out and cut my hand on some glass. It almost killed me because I burst an artery and ripped a tendon. I lost so much blood. When the nurses told me I could have died, I fainted. I still have no feeling in two of my fingers although I can still move them.

STEPHEN SIMMONS (Hearts, Dunfermline, Raith Rovers): The Hearts players had a Christmas night out in Glasgow and started drinking at lunchtime. Elvis had booked a function suite at the Marriot hotel but by the time we got there for our meal, everyone was absolutely steaming. We all started chucking things at each other like forks, spoons and bread rolls. There was a guy with his karaoke equipment but he left after four songs because it was just mayhem. Stephane Mahe was at the centre of a lot of it. He was a madman.

JIM PATERSON: In my first year at Motherwell, we went down to Newcastle from the Saturday until the Monday. I remember sitting in a quiet bar where there were only the players, another bloke and the barmaid. Paul Quinn came bursting in with a balaclava and a fake gun. The barmaid was absolutely terrified and the guy sitting at the bar almost did a John Smeaton and was ready to go for him. We knew it was Paul though as he had done the same thing earlier in the day.

DAVE BAIKIE (ex-Arbroath and Cowdenbeath boss and Juniors supremo): When I was manager at Cowdenbeath, the players barricaded me in my room when we were in a hotel in England. The boys had been at a disco and when they came back in the early hours, they stuck about forty chairs at the door and I couldn't get out. I found out Liam Buchanan was one of the instigators so the coaching staff blocked him in his room as revenge.

DAVID ELEBERT (Irish defender at Hamilton): At a Christmas night out, Mark McLaughlin ended up carrying me to my hotel bedroom because I was so drunk I passed out in a toilet cubicle where he found me.

CRAIG SAMSON: I snuck out of the hotel while on Scotland Under-21 duty and was put in a cell overnight. We were staying in Kilmarnock and a few of us decided to sneak out on the Saturday night. We were in a nightclub but got into a row with the bouncers and the police intervened. I wouldn't shut up and then they started jogging over to us. Andy Dowie told me to run but I didn't and I was put in the cells, although I was never charged. I was dropped from the next squad but I managed to get back in again.

Crazy Fool!

THERE are your dafties but then there are your utter idiots who will try anything once. But these are the guys who give a dressing room their togetherness and spirit. Just don't try these at home!

MARTYN CORRIGAN (Falkirk, Motherwell, Partick): Big Yogi Hughes is a real character. I'd just signed for Falkirk and I was walking through the gym when I saw Yogi with a weight sellotaped to his privates. I asked him what he was doing and he said: "This is how it gets bigger."

KENNY ARTHUR (Partick keeper and intelligent): On my first day at Partick, the boys told me I had to go to the gaffer's room to get my boots as that's where they were kept. I was quite nervous. I knocked on the door and went in and behind this cloud of smoke was John Lambie, who just said: "Who the **** are you?" I just stood there in silence not knowing what to say. I didn't even get my boots.

DES MCKEOWN (Football journeyman and *SunSport* columnist): I moved out to overtake a car near Kilsyth and the idiot started speeding up and slowing down, refusing to let me in, one way or another, even though I was racing for a head-on collision with an oncoming bus. I was so furious I decided to follow him. He tried to pull a fly one by racing ahead and pulling into a cul-de-sac where he lay down on the seat and turned off his lights. I parked my car at the bottom of the street and walked towards his vehicle. Suddenly he roared the engine into life but I was determined he wouldn't get away and jumped on his bonnet. He swerved and ended up throwing me into a hedge where I lay with blood running down my hands, a windscreen wiper in one and an aerial in the other.

MICHAEL GARDYNE (Laugh-a-minute nutter at Ross County): Up at Ross County, Martin 'Jimmy' Scott would shave every part of his body, including his legs and armpits. He'd even carry on shaving when the boss walked into the changing room. The boy is a nutter. Dean Keenan would come into the Cappielow dressing room, shouting "Hulk Hogan" then rip his t-shirt off.

GEORGE MCCLUSKEY: We were on a pre-season trip to Holland and on a four-hour bus ride when Frank McGarvey and Johnny Doyle spent the whole time kid-on fighting. They were so exhausted they couldn't play the game. Johnny was nuts and loved to wind Rangers fans up. After beating them at Ibrox, we were outside the stadium when Andy Cameron walked out. Johnny mooned at him.

DEREK MCINNES (Rangers, Dundee United and top young boss at St Johnstone): A few of us were out at his place one afternoon and after a few beers Paul Gascoigne brought out an air gun. He told Jimmy Five Bellies he'd give him twenty seconds to run away and then he'd start shooting. For every pellet Gazza hit him with, he'd give Jimmy £50. Jimmy ran away but Gazza started shooting after about eight seconds, hitting Jimmy in the a**e with about a dozen shots. As far as I know, Gazza paid up.

DARREN SHERIDAN (Clyde, St Johnstone): I once dressed up as a madman with an axe in the village we were staying in while I was at Leeds. I put on a wig, a cloak and carried a four-foot axe and walked about the village. People just drove on when they saw me and no one would come near me. People were terrified and there were two guys in a pub who got really scared. In the end, cops in four police cars went to our digs and asked the players who was dressed up, but they never caught me.

SCOTT MCLEAN: When I went for my first driving test, I had trouble reading the registration plate of a car because my contact lenses were giving me bother. The instructor went to get a measuring tape and I went over to the car to memorise the number. When the instructor came out, the owner of the car came out too and drove off. Suffice to say I failed.

LEE MAIR: We call big Lee Wilkie 'Streakie' because he is a big streak of p***. He's had that nickname for as long as I've known.

He is a bit crazy. He would come to training with big rockets which fire about 180-feet into the air and then a parachute guy falls out. He also came in with remote control cars and all sorts of other toys – although to be fair to him, the rest of the guys played with the toys too.

JOHN HUGHES: Ian McCall is daft as a brush. Once we were golfing in Marbella and he hit a ball through the window of his buggy. He'd have got away with it if he had parked without anyone noticing, but he crashed into a wall and there was uproar. Another time, we were out for a pint and I could smell burning. He'd set fire to my shirt, which was hanging out the back of my trousers, and the lads had to put it out with their pints.

STEVE PATERSON: Scott McLean once ran a lap of Caley Stadium naked for a £12 bet unbeknown to him that the chairman and I were up in the hospitality box watching him. We were in stitches but we promptly fined him because we had to be seen not to condone his actions. Another time Trigger was spotted in a karaoke bar in Inverness with his top off and a curly wig singing a Tom Jones song. But he wasn't with any mates and just wanted to enter the competition – that sums him up.

LEE MAKEL (Hearts, Livingston, Dunfermline): Paul Gascoigne used to drive around in a tractor and churn up the fields we were training in with Newcastle. He did it all the time and the grounds-man Davie said if he did it again he would set his Alsatian dog Max on to him. Gazza didn't believe him. But sure enough, the next time he did it, out came Max. Gazza practically wet himself. He ended up on the roof of a car to escape!

PETER HETHERSTON (Raith Rovers, Airdrie): A good friend of mine Jim Cowell, whom I played with at Falkirk, is the biggest liar I have ever come across. He is the only guy who can tell a lie and prove it. We were arguing in the pub one night and he told us his two kids were born in a private hospital. We ended up phoning his wife at three in the morning to prove him wrong.

CAMPBELL MONEY (St Mirren legend): Billy Abercrombie wasn't so much crazy as daft. I remember one time he went to take his dog for a walk, tied it to a lamp post and wasn't seen for five days. But he was still St Mirren's captain and he was a big inspiration, especially when we won the cup.

CHRIS STRAIN (Ayr United): David Lowing makes me look like a monk. He would put extra money away for Magaluf in case he needed bailed out. He's Jekyll and Hyde, one minute telling you how much he loves puppies, then punching doors to work himself up for games. His nickname is 'Psycho'.

STEVIE TOSH: Craig Barr genuinely thinks it's someone's job to turn on the cats' eyes on the road when it gets dark. He's also the boy who, when a game was called off at Livingston because of a flooded pitch, asked the question: "Do they not have undersoil heating?" Tube.

GERRY COLLINS: On Comic Relief Day, Allan Moore stuck a Red Nose on the end of his you know what and started swinging it round and round. Aggie came in and warned: "I'm going to tell your wife."

WILLIE FALCONER (Aberdeen, Celtic, Dundee, Watford): David James was No.2 to Tony Cotton when I was at Watford and I had to room with him. The thing was, David used to take fits in his sleep and completely wreck rooms. The other thing is that no one warned me about this – even though he'd been known to knock people out with flying punches – and I got the fright of my life when he went off on one. I remember hiding in the toilet of my hotel room one night while he was going mental.

DAVIE IRONS: John Lambie's team talks were brilliant. We played Rangers at Firhill and he had trouble pronouncing Alexei Mikhailitchenko. After about five attempts, he gave up and just said "that Russian b*****d".

PAUL MCGRILLEN: Scott McLean travelled down to Blackpool with wet clothes in a bin liner. I have no idea why but I think he just took them out the wash and stuck them in a bag. He took his stuff out and put it on a radiator to dry off – he didn't seem to mind the creases but looked a state. The guy is bonkers.

MICKY WEIR (Hibs legend): John 'Budgie' Burridge was a lunatic. He would always leave his motorbike at Waverley Station when he went down to Newcastle. Andy Gray told me that when he went to the Burridges' for dinner, all of a sudden Budgie's wife would throw apples and oranges at him without warning to keep him on his toes.

KEVIN TINDAL (Prison officer and footballer): One time, Bradley Kerr put some Ralgex in Jimmy Fotheringham's boxers so Jimmy heated a spoon on a cooker and put it on Bradley's neck. It stuck to his neck and left a big burn mark – the joke went a bit too far.

RUSSELL DUNCAN (Aberdeen, Caley Thistle): When I was about sixteen, Ryan Esson, Lee Barclay and I decided to take the minibus at Aberdeen for a spin. I only took it down the street but then there was a crunching sound and when I took the key out the ignition, the engine kept running. The boys thought that was pretty funny. We ended up having to pay £2,500 to repair the engine. They took £50 out of our wages every month – I don't know if we actually paid it all. When we were being grilled over the minibus at Aberdeen, I was saying that it wasn't us while Ryan was in the other room saying it was me.

SCOTT MCCULLOCH (Dundee United, Dunfermline, Partick Thistle): Gerry Britton and George Shaw were always at it at Dunfermline. They would basically try and outdo each other with practical jokes. We had a new hairdryer installed and George was the only one who used it because he was concerned about his receding hairline. Gerry knew this so he tampered with the dryer and when George turned it on, it exploded in his hands.

KENNY ARTHUR: Chic Charnley used to terrorise poor Andy Gibson who had a bit of a funny toe. His foot looked like a golf club so Chic would end up calling him 'One Wood Foot' and said he could hit a ball a mile with it.

SCOTT HIGGINS (Aussie Falkirk keeper): Tom Willis is another keeper at Queensland. When we played Perth away we had a night out and the coaches found Tom stark naked lying on a couch in the hotel foyer. They couldn't wake him up. He had no idea where his clothes had gone, had lost his wallet and phone and claimed he must have been mugged.

BRYAN PRUNTY: There was a lad at Celtic called David 'Spud' Murphy who was from Ireland. He'd be standing at a bar in a pub pouring pints over his head while he was still sober.

JOHN BURRIDGE (King of the lunatics): I sat on the cross-bar during a match for Crystal Palace. We were playing Ipswich and were 3–0 up with five minutes to go, so I climbed up onto the bar. I was shouting: "I've got the best seat in the house lads – you get some view from up here!" An Ipswich player tried a shot from forty yards and I had to jump down to smother the ball. The crowd burst out laughing and our boss Terry Venables loved it.

DAVID PROCTOR: It'll come as no surprise when I say Scott Brown from my time at Hibs is the daftest I know. The YTS boys were in Tenerife on holiday when we hired mopeds. Scott didn't realise you parked them outside – he took the moped in through the lobby, into the lift and into his room.

STEPHEN SWIFT (Lower league scallywag): We were in Stockholm in Sweden for Kevin Gaughan's stag do and Michael Moore was chatting to the most stunning woman in the place. I don't know how. She asked him where he was from and he just said: "Foxbar." He didn't say Glasgow or Scotland, he just expected her to know this obscure place in Paisley. We absolutely slaughtered him for it but he says he still took her back to his room. We don't believe him.

CRAIG SAMSON: Back when I was with Ross County, Michael Gardyne decided he wanted to be wrapped up in tape while he was in the physio room. He was wrapped up below the knees and while he was walking down the corridor, I pushed him and he fell and smashed his face. Scott Leitch was cracking up at me, but Michael stupidly told him it was his own idea.

ALAN MCINALLY: We had lost in Austria to Rapid Vienna and Frank McGarvey and Murdo MacLeod scrapped on the bus after some words, but got into a clinch and fell on to the floor. But neither of them let go. The players stepped over them to get off the bus and the two dopey b*****ds were still lying there refusing to give up.

MARK CAMPBELL (Falkirk, Ayr, Raith): We used to take turns at driving to training and matches at Falkirk and Neil Scally turned up in his uncle's work van with a ladder on it. His uncle is an alarm fitter, so he borrowed it. I wouldn't have put it past him that he was out trying to sell alarms.

SCOTT CHAPLAIN (Ayr, Partick, Dumbarton): Most people have heard the story about John Hughes punching the referee's door after he was sent off at Somerset. But what people don't know is he went into the home dressing room and put his foot through the wooden bench and got his foot stuck.

MIKE FRASER: Mark Brown and I used to do extra training and we would take the minibus to the local park. But we shouldn't have because we weren't twenty-five years old, which you need to be to drive them. I crashed into a wall when I went too wide going through a mini-roundabout and I damaged the side, causing thousands of pounds worth of damage. Luckily, Craig Brewster wasn't too angry with us.

GARY MCSWEGAN (Rangers, Dundee United, Hearts, Kilmarnock): We were having a pre-match meal in Kilmarnock and they were showing a Manchester United game. Andy McLaren went up behind the screen and all you could see was his shadow – he jumped around pretending he was playing in the game.

JIM BALLANTYNE (Airdrie chairman and SFL president): Willie McLaren certainly took the p*** – he was always off because one of his grannies died. I swear he must have had about four of them judging by the times he used that excuse.

ALEX RAE (Hardman): When I was at Falkirk, one of my own players, Colin McNair, deliberately tackled me in midfield. I was running and he just took the ball off me and said: "I'm the f*****g playmaker in this team." The two of us just burst out laughing.

RYAN MCCANN: My mate Ross Murray, on a whim, decided to drive his wrecked Rover Metro from Blantyre to Beijing. He went with a couple of mates and they ended up writing the car off in the Gobi desert in Mongolia. They ended up relying on some locals to get them transport to China.

CHRIS JARDINE: A night out with my mate Craig Allen can be a pretty strange experience as he is the strangest drunk ever. He once punched my mate and I in the face completely out the blue. He still can't remember it to this day so we still don't know why.

DON HUTCHISON: We had some great Christmas nights out at Liverpool. I remember John Barnes in Ku Klux Klan gear. Jamie Redknapp and I would do a variation of Batman and Robin called Fatman and Blobbin.

TAM SCOBBIE (Falkirk Bairn): Our welfare and development officer Ross Wilson was sitting at his desk when John Hughes stripped naked and sat on him. Ross ran out of the room. John also pretended to our new signing Scott Flinders that he was in fact the kit-man and the kit-man Cheb was the manager, which was hilarious because he believed him.

WILLIE MILLER: We were set to go on a tour of Iran, Australia and New Zealand with Aberdeen and Doug Rougvie turned up at the airport with the biggest suitcase filled with cornflakes, rashers of bacon and tomato sauce thinking you couldn't get food in these places.

ARTHUR NUMAN: Fernando Ricksen was called 'Psycho' so that says it all. He was so hyper the whole day and had ADHD. His eyes were always wide open and I didn't like being near him when he had a drink in him. I remember him hanging from curtains in a hotel lobby and heading traffic signs.

JOHN MCMASTER: Sharing a room with Doug Rougvie was scary. He was a draughtsman at the time and I hid his exam papers from him one night. He asked me where they were and I told him he must have dropped them. He just lifted me up and my feet were dangling. It was the worst thing I've ever done in my life.

BOBBY LINN (Dundee, Peterhead, East Fife): Dean Keenan is the thickest boy I have ever seen. We were playing a game with Morton and when we went for our pre-match meal, there was a bowling area in the hotel. I remember coming downstairs and spotted Deano lying face down, saying: "Hurry up and bowl," – the boys were smashing bowls off his head and he's still got the two big bumps on his head to this day.

PAUL KINNAIRD (Journeyman and dressing room legend): I went to Shrewsbury but never got on with their manager John

Bond. I got so fed up with him that, one day at Doncaster, I decided to rattle the ball into the dugout because he was wearing a white mackintosh. It flew about in there like a pinball and the mud went everywhere. He told me not to come back.

SIMON LYNCH: I'm sorry wee man, but the daftest player who was at Airdrie is Kevin Watt. He once asked if Lance Armstrong was the guy who landed on the moon!

DUNCAN SHEARER (Hairy Highlander with Blackburn, Aberdeen and Scotland): I remember we were about to play Celtic and John Burridge just sat naked in the dressing room with just his gloves on while we all sat in our kits. Willie Miller came in for the team talk, glanced over at 'Budgie' and just shook his head.

DEREK ADAMS (Ross County): When he was at Livingston, Martin 'Jimmy' Scott asked the then manager Paul Lambert if Livi were able to stay in the SPL, could he receive his Rolex watch as a bonus so he could pawn it and use the money to buy double glazing for his house.

WILLIE KINNIBURGH: We were on Stevie Hammell's stag do in Magaluf when we decided to see who could hit a punch-bag the hardest. I swung for it, missed, hit the post behind it and broke my hand. It had swollen up but I did nothing until I got back to Scotland. Bizarrely, when I was in hospital, in walked Stevie, as he had been bitten by something and his hand was swollen.

ANNE-MARIE BALLANTYNE (Airdrie secretary and Jim's sister): Stephen McKeown borrowed my golf clubs and played a round complete with my hat, gloves and even my lipstick.

DANNY GRAINGER: Craig Conway, Jon Daly and I just became idiots when we were together and having a drink. We had a few at the end of the season and ended up smashing a guitar over each other's heads. Jon decided to trample all over my fiancée's head as well – so that didn't go down too well.

5

Daftie!

FOOTBALLERS are talented – but they do lack some common sense at times. Maybe it's heading the ball which has killed all the brain cells. The following examples explain a lot.

IAN CAMPBELL (Former Brechin manager and twin brother of Dick): I got dressed up as Boy George for a party but forgot I was meeting the Montrose secretary to go on loan for a month. You will never see a more surprised individual ever!

SCOTT McCULLOCH: I was driving up with Marc Smyth from Ayrshire when we passed some Highland cows. Marc said: "Bob, what are they?" I told him they were Highland coos and he said: "Oh, I thought they were buffalo." I'm not kidding, he was serious. He really gives Irish people a bad name.

EAMONN BANNON: Rab Prentice at Hearts wasn't the brightest. He took his driving test and to indicate in those days you would stick your hand out the window if you were turning right – and to turn left, you flapped your right arm. But as Rab turned left he stuck out his left arm and hit the driving instructor in the face.

MARC TWADDLE: Paul Cairney, who had just arrived from Queen's Park, makes some pretty outrageous statements. Gary Harkins, Ryan McStay and Mark Roberts were all having a carry-on with him and Paul turned round and said: "You're a pair of d***s!" We were all rolling about laughing. We call him "Bobby Boucher" after the character from *The Waterboy*.

GARY MCDONALD: It hasn't taken me long to figure out how daft Zander Diamond is. Some of the stuff that comes out of his mouth, I don't know where it comes from. He was doing TV when he was injured for the home game against Rangers. At half time he was asked how the game was going and he said: "I don't think the boys can play any badder!" He's just inventing words now. It is even on Youtube.

CRAIG BROWN (Former Scotland manager): We were in Athens and Ally McCoist got a minibus to go to the Acropolis. One player, reputed to be Duncan Ferguson, asked where we were going. When we told him, he said: "I didn't know the discos were open in the afternoon!" When McCoist said it was a place of historical interest, Dunc replied: "Once you've seen one Acropolis, you've seen the lot."

GARY HARKINS (Partick, Dundee): Shaun Dillon is from another planet. My pals and I were sitting in his house one night when we asked him to turn down his heating as it was absolutely roasting. He said he couldn't so we looked at each other and asked him why not. He then told us he doesn't control his heating, so we asked him who did. He told us that NASA satellites controlled his heating.

CRAIG MCKEOWN: Alex Williams has to be the daftest person I know. We were doing some running at Broadwood when Joe Miller asked where Alex was. I walked into the changing room to find him bent over banging the toilet door against his head repeatedly. I asked him what he was doing and he said he was trying to get out of doing the running and was making it look like he'd fainted.

BRYAN HODGE (Partick): Paul Cairney tried to put a two-pronged plug for his iPod into a three-hole socket. He was actually trying to force it in.

CALLUM MACDONALD (Peterhead): We heard a story about Andrew Bagshaw that when he was playing for the Scotland youth team he complained of a sore foot at half time. When the physio rolled his sock down, his hotel key fell out. He had been playing the whole game with it in his sock.

ALAN GOW (Airdrie, Falkirk, Rangers, Hibs): When the big tsunami disaster happened, they had these wristbands in aid of it.

When we were getting our photo taken at Airdrie with the wristbands on, Marvyn Wilson asked Willie what was going on. Willie looked at his wristband and said: "It's for the Tunisia appeal!"

STUART MCCAFFREY (Caley Thistle, St Johnstone): Barry Robson came into training at Caley one day and announced that he had signed a PRENUPTIAL agreement with Dundee United. We all knew he had meant to say PRE-CONTRACT agreement and the whole dressing room was in stitches.

SCOTT STRUTHERS (Hamilton Accies secretary and Hamilton Palace frequenter): We have had a good few over the years. Before we beat Brechin 4-3, we stopped off in Forfar and Dylan Kerr came back with a Ruud Gullit wig. He was going to get one of the young lads to keep it for him behind the goal in case he scored. I knew he would get booked so I made sure it didn't happen.

ALEX TOTTEN (Ex-Falkirk boss): I asked one player at Falkirk – who shall remain nameless – his date of birth. He said it was December 20. I asked him what year and he replied: "Every year." I was also in signing talks with Sergei Baltacha at St Johnstone. He said he wanted a car as part of the deal. I thought he would want a Mercedes but he asked for a LADA. He was proud to drive it around.

MARK ROBERTS: When Martin Glancy heard that Julie Fleeting had signed for Ross County he thought she was going to play for the actual men's first-team. He was asking questions like: "Do you think that she will score goals?" and "What is she going to do about the showers?" Unbelievable.

STUART TAYLOR: There was a Welsh player at Drogheda called Chris Todd who did stupid things like go into a fish shop and say: "Look at all the erotic fish."

DAVIE NICHOLLS (Clydebank, Falkirk, Gretna): My pre-season trick at Clydebank was to pull my trousers down, pull my pants up tight and march about like a baboon.

RONNIE MACDONALD (Hamilton owner): There was a player called David Findlay who I had at Knightswood Juveniles. We had a throw-in set-piece move for a cup final one year and it went wrong. David found himself in the clear in the box and he stopped suddenly and shouted: "Hey, I was supposed to be the decoy." Another time, we played a side that had their sponsor's name Lafferty's emblazoned on their shoulders. I said to him: "Pick up the big lad Lafferty at a corner." The corner came, he saw eight guys with the same name and said to Allan Maitland: "They've got a hell of a lot of Lafferty's in this team."

MARK MCNALLY (Celtic, Stirling Albion): There's only one man from outer space – Scott McLean. And he would prove it every day. He is the only man I know who will try to eat a Pot Noodle cold. The kettle was on the blink, so he tried cold water and munched his way through the pot. He also wears contact lenses and is always forgetting them. He's some boy.

ALAN COMBE (St Mirren, Dundee United, Kilmarnock): When I was at St Mirren, I used to share a flat with Barry McLaughlin. He was a great guy and incredibly intelligent but from time to time he became a bit doolally. One night we went to a quiz in Paisley. He parked the car and left it for a few hours. When it finished we went out to find the car with the keys still in the ignition and the engine running. It's a wonder it wasn't stolen but then who'd want to nick a clapped-out Ford Fiesta anyway?

STEPHEN SWIFT: My pal is Dexy Wingate, who played at Stranraer and I also played with him at Benburb. McDonald's sponsored Benburb and he told me that I would get free meals, so I took a guy from my work and went in and pointed to the picture of the team on the wall telling them that it was me and asking for free food. But they said no and my work-mate had to pay for it.

JIM STEWART (Rangers, Scotland): One boy at Kilmarnock, who I won't name, actually thought oil was invented by a single person. We kept him going and he believed that this one guy made a fortune by selling it to everyone else. That shows you the level of intelligence they have. They were a close-knit group of three or four thick guys and they know who they are. It wasn't Kris Boyd though – compared to the ones I'm on about, he's a genius.

STEVIE TOSH: Aberdeen were playing Ajax in a pre-season friendly in Portugal. Steve Paterson forgot his whiteboard so wrote the team on the dressing room wall. It had just been painted white and he'd done it in permanent ink. The best thing was he wrote Phil McGuire's name twice and had to scrawl over it. Only Pele.

JIM DUFFY: One of the players was telling everyone his wife was due to give birth at any moment. Wee Iain Anderson asked how long she'd been pregnant for. He also thought women were pregnant for longer if they were having twins.

BOBBY MANN (Forfar, Caley Thistle, Dundee, Peterhead): Wee David Bagan came into training and claimed he'd seen a UFO. He was driving past Aviemore on the way to Inverness and insisted there was a bright light in the sky. When it was suggested to him that it might have been one of the ski lifts he went pretty quiet.

JAMIE MCKENZIE (Partick): At Thistle, there was a boy called Brian Smith, the thickest lad I think it's possible to meet. He went in to see John McVeigh one day to ask if he could get a new pair of boots, and John asked him what size he was. Brian didn't know though and said he was either a seven or an eight. The gaffer couldn't believe it and said he had to be one or the other. He asked him: "What size of shoes do you take?" and Brian answered: "Why, am I getting a new pair of shoes as well?"

PAUL LOVERING (Hibs, Ayr, Airdrie): As a qualified motor mechanic, this is pretty stupid. I was coming back from Perth one day from training at St Johnstone when I accidentally filled my petrol car up with diesel. I thought I'd got away with it but sure enough we broke down twenty minutes later. I had to phone my brother Richard for a tow.

MARK CRILLY (Shyness at Ayr): I was on a train travelling back to Paisley from Ayr with John Bradford when we decided to doctor our weekly pass. Mine ran out on the 8th so I stuck a one in front of it to make it the 18th. John's ran out on the 28th but he said he would change it to the 38th. I looked at him and he said: "What? You think I can't do it?"

GREG SHIELDS: Noel Hunt would tell a different story every day. He would say he has a cousin who can cure blindness by using peppers. He used to talk about his dog – the one that ran away – and how it would catch flying ducks. And he also says his house is haunted because every time the Domino's Pizza man comes round his front door is always open. He even says when he goes to bed at night his bed has switched sides the next morning.

MARTYN CORRIGAN: When Motherwell went to Lanzarote, Paul Harvey didn't put any suntan lotion on. He claimed he didn't need it, but we just watched him get redder and redder. He went back to his room, got up in the middle of the night, fell asleep on the toilet and broke his nose on the bidet. He was found in the morning, out cold with sunstroke and a smashed nose.

GARY ARBUCKLE: Craig Bryson has the mental age of seven. His favourite joke is: "What is red and hard to eat? A piece and fire engine."

FRANK MCAVENNIE: I went on Wogan with Denis Law just before I was about to make my Scotland debut. I was about to have a go at Terry because he said my gran would be watching the show up in St Mirren, thinking it was a place. I was just thinking: "You idiot!"

GARY DEMPSEY (Dunfermline, Aberdeen): At Dunfermline, Noel Hunt and I shared digs together. We would usually get our laundry done but one time we had to go and do it ourselves. Noel went in with our gear and we were to pick it up the next day. I gave him £20 and waited in the car but he then came running out saying they wanted £180. It turned out we put the clothes in for dry cleaning and it was about £4 for each item. It was more than what the clothes were worth.

CHRIS KILLEN: The kit-room staff locked me in the club reception for a few hours. There was a list of numbers on the receptionist's phone. I tried them all but they were just office numbers. Everyone was out because it was an away game. I was one call away from the police before someone let me out.

SIMON MENSING: I was invited to the bingo and I thought I had all the numbers so I shouted: "House!" The whole place stopped and the guy came over to check my numbers but I didn't have one of them. I was so embarrassed because there were hundreds of people there. I haven't been back.

RICHARD GORDON (BBC *Sportsound* presenter): Jim Spence, on air, thought he'd got locked in a toilet at Parkhead and was banging on the door shouting for help. He was too short to see the 'No Exit' sign and hadn't realised it was a one-way system.

PAUL MATHERS (Veteran keeper): Dean Keenan at Morton was the kind of guy who would come in with his hair bleached and one time he came in with his goatee beard bleached. Graham Stewart came to a game after spending too long on the sun-bed and was bright red. He could barely play when he came on as sub and appeared in *SunSport* posing in pictures. He also peed from the top of a car the night we won promotion.

STEVIE MURRAY (Kilmarnock, Partick): Mark Roberts is an idiot. The boy is a legend but he'd give an Askit a sore head.

CRAIG CONWAY (Dundee United Scottish Cup hero): I once drove to the completely wrong airport to pick up my girlfriend Kristy from holiday.

DAVE BAIKIE: Grant Paterson at Tayport used to come up with some really bizarre excuses for being late or missing training. I remember once he told me that he had a dental appointment – at 8pm! At East Fife, Jonathan Smart once told us his dog had swallowed his car key. That one has got to be up there with the best of them.

DAVID ELEBERT: Well, the craziest thing I ALMOST did was get my nipple pierced. We were on our end-of-season trip to Magaluf when Tom Parratt and I went into a place to get it done as we thought it would be a great thing to get done at the time. We had a look around but then we both chickened out and ran out of the place.

CRAIG SAMSON: Kris Boyd is the thickest guy I know. I remember one time he wanted to go on the computer and asked me how you spell MSN! When I told him, "M . . . S . . . N," he started to back pedal and tried to make out he was kidding.

MARK CAMPBELL: It was coming up to Bonfire Night, Gary Teale brought fireworks into the Ayr dressing room to sell. I don't know where he got them from. Neil Scally also came in with a silver knife set as well. He was selling them for weeks – they were very popular.

DAVID ROWSON (Aberdeen, Partick): I was playing for Aberdeen in a game against Rangers at Ibrox when Paul Gascoigne scored a hat trick. It was a roasting day and when I tried to spit, it dribbled down my chin – what I didn't realise was that the camera was focusing on me at the time and you could see clearly what had happened. My dad had taped it and it was embarrassing to see. I got a lot of stick from my mates as well.

CALLUM MACDONALD: The Peterhead boys played a prank on one of the younger lads Andrew Bagshaw. Someone told him

Asda has a singles night between 7-8pm on a Friday night. We kept this going for weeks and he kept going on about it, telling everyone. I think he went a couple of times.

ROBBIE RAESIDE: The daftest person I know is Brian Scott. He looked at the team-sheet for a game against Dumbarton and said they had a hit-man in their line-up. It actually said kit-man! We pointed out that a car parked in the corner of the ground at Albion Rovers for a disabled spectator was actually a prize for the man of the match. Brian believed us and had a stormer, scoring twice.

ANNE-MARIE BALLANTYNE: Mark Roberts drove me insane because he would always have some sort of story. He also had no problem in calling me at 5am when he was out to see if I could get him a taxi. One player, who shall remain nameless, was asked when he arrived at training in pre-season in Belfast if he had any gear and replied: "Not on me but if you let me know what you want I'll get it for you."

DON HUTCHISON: I was playing for Sheffield United against Ipswich in the play-offs. We were on the bus when I climbed out of the skylight at the back, crawled along the roof while the bus was travelling at 30mph and jumped down on Howard Kendall from the front skylight. He absolutely s**t himself.

GERRY MCCABE: I played alongside Jim Kean at Clyde . . . and talk about daft. He was having a shocker one day and Craig Brown went mental at half time, asking him what was wrong. Jim told him it was because the wind kept blowing his collar up and poking him in the eye. Craig tucked his collar inside his shirt.

ADAM COAKLEY: Dean Keenan is the daftest I know. He has no limits and is bonkers. On my first night out with him, he stripped naked coming out of a club and then jumped in a bin. Strangers took out their phones and took pictures. I was told that is what he does all the time.

6

Dish the Dirt

THERE is nothing like a secret being let out the bag. Who wants the rest of the world to know you shave all your body hair? There are no hiding places when it comes to the A to Z as players spill the beans on their team-mates.

SCOTT MURRAY: I played with Dwight Yorke at Aston Villa and I used to get porn from him. He had a box full of videos stashed under his stairs.

DEREK FLEMING (Livingston, Partick, Hamilton): Scott Crabbe fancied me when I was in drag. He held a party at his house and I dressed up as a woman with a blonde wig, suspenders . . . the works. I walked up to his door and I swear he thought I was a bird. You could see his eyes popping out. He was disappointed when he realised it was me, but the more drink he and Andy Seaton had, the more they wanted a piece of me!

DEREK TOWNSLEY: Kenny Deuchar and Ryan McGuffie must surely be secret lovers! I'm telling you, they cannot be separated. If you have an argument with one of them, the other will pipe up and defend him. It goes beyond friendship. They bonded because they have both been students.

ALEX WILLIAMS: I caught Craig McKeown and Stevie Masterton catching a kip in my bed at a hotel. Their legs were tangled up and somebody's hand was touching the other's ear. It was like Steve Martin and John Candy in *Planes, Trains and Automobiles*.

JAMIE LANGFIELD (Dundee, Aberdeen): Lee Wilkie is prone to sleep-walking. I'd hate to be sharing a room with him if he does because he ends up punching holes in walls or taking out light bulbs. He once got up, moved a wardrobe and punched a big hole in the wall before going back to bed.

WILLIE KINNIBURGH: At Partick, Ian Maxwell and Marc Twaddle said they are penis twins. They claim their privates are identical and look like dolphins.

MICHAEL GARDYNE: At Queen's Park, Ryan Holms was known as 'Jobby'. When we went to Germany in pre-season we had a luminous orange suit called the Jobby Suit for the worst trainer and Ryan was in it every day for the full week.

JIM PATERSON: Some of the Motherwell boys like to play the Xbox and they play online with people around the country.

Martyn Corrigan, David Clarkson, Marc Fitzpatrick and Simon Mensing would call themselves 'The Warlords' when they play a war game called *Call of Duty*. They actually go around training shouting: "We are the Warlords." They'll even team up together in five-a-side games. It's very sad.

ROBERT CONNOR (Dundee, Aberdeen): There was no pleasing Alex Ferguson and he would have ridiculous fines for players. One time he fined John Hewitt because he overtook him on the way into training.

JOHN HUGHES: When I played at Hibs, I would call the two groundsmen at Hibs, Tam McCourt and Darren Coyle, Billy and Johnny after the characters from Hale and Pace. I would come into the ground and go: "Hello Billy, hello Johnny!" They gave it so much stick and were up to the dodges. Tam looks like Alain Robidoux the snooker player ... while Darren is the spitting image of Oliver Hardy.

LEE WILKIE: Every time I would meet Steven Thompson on a night out in Dundee, he would grab me and lick my face. I don't know what he was playing at but he is a character and I get on with him because we were both in the Scotland Under-21s together. But he needs to get his problem sorted out.

ANDY MCLAREN: Big Kris Boyd needs to go on the *The Jerry Springer Show* – the lad was just bonkers at Kilmarnock. Every time he took a shot he made sound effects with it like "Vooooooooooom!"

He definitely comes from another planet and I think I am the only person who can relate to him.

CHRIS HILLCOAT: Hamilton's secretary Scott Struthers would have a few stories about this dungeon at his place, which he calls a pantry. He keeps a lot of his football stuff in it but we would kid him on that he must have shackle sessions down there with his girlfriends.

SCOTT MURRAY. Sharing a shower with my old Fraserburgh boss Charlie Duncan is a strange experience. He is the hairiest man I have ever seen and we call him 'The Ape'! He does a trick in the shower where he tosses up a bar of soap, traps it with his foot and flicks it on to the back of his neck. Some people can't do that with a football.

STEVIE FERGUSON (Ross County): Alex Bone once collapsed with exhaustion during a game and had to be taken off because his eyes were rolling. The doctor sent him home but when Neale Cooper went to check on him later in the evening Boney was already changed and out on the town.

CRAIG FARNAN (Brechin City): There was a reserve keeper at East Fife called Craig Martin who was really annoying because he always talked about sex. I travelled with him and Jim Butter to and from Dundee. Jim and I would have bets on how long it took Craig to mention something sexual – usually it was thirty seconds. We called him 'Harry the Hormone'.

CRAIG HINCHCLIFFE (Arbroath, St Mirren, Partick Thistle): I can imagine Craig Feroz saying he is a woman, which wouldn't surprise me. There's something not quite right about him. He's very bubbly but he went to a Bruce Springsteen concert in Paris with a stars and stripes bandana!

DAVIE NICHOLLS: Graeme Connell is a gent but he would do your head in with his set routines. He eats a banana at the same time, goes to the toilet at the same time and must eat his dinner at a set time. Scott 'Nipper' Thomson blows your hair off with his gas attacks.

TAM MCMANUS (Hibs, Dundee): Big 'Yogi' Hughes was mental when he was at Hibs. He gave every single player a nickname. He used to call me 'Julius Caesar' claiming I had the same haircut. Paul Lovering was 'John Merrick', Paul Hartley was 'Mowgli' out of the Jungle Book and Mixu Paatelainen was 'Melon Head'.

CHRIS MCGROARTY: I would always call Scott Thomson 'Heid' because he has got a massive napper – I'd like Mulder and Scully to investigate. He would always call me 'Pea-heid' because mine is so tiny. My old school buddy David McGuire, who was at Airdrie, had the funniest name. He was called 'Quack' for some reason – I think it's because he spoke like a duck as a kid.

STEVIE TOSH: One of the young lads, Stephen Craig, got a letter from a fan that was too disgusting to print in detail. It had all sorts of sexual remarks in it and I could see his eyes lighting up until he got to the bottom of the note. It said: "P.S. I'm a gay man." We were in stitches and I think one of the lads had done a good job of winding Stephen up.

MARK BURCHILL (Celtic, Dunfermline, Kilmarnock): Jim Lauchlan has the funniest patter I've ever heard. He's even got his own catchphrase – "Check out the clobber" – because he is heavily into buying expensive clothes. He also says: "If it hasn't got a name it doesn't get in my wardrobe."

CRAIG DARGO (Raith Rovers, Kilmarnock, St Mirren): Ian Cameron is without a doubt the brainiest footballer I've come across. The man has so much knowledge. Ask him about anything and he will give you an answer in great detail. He is an accountant and you can tell. We'd all come into training with *The Sun* and he'd be sitting at a table studying the *Financial Times*. The dumbest is definitely Marvin Andrews. He was doing a puzzle in the programme and spelled fruit F-R-I-U-T. He took some stick, I can tell you.

GLYNN HURST (Ayr): I don't know anyone who needs it but John Davies is a walking advert for Viagra. He looks good in anything. He could wear a pair of ten-year-old wellies and still look good enough to have all the women swooning over him.

CRAIG BREWSTER (Dundee United legend): The funniest thing I've ever seen in football was whenever Scott 'Nipper'

Thomson took his top off trying to show what I wouldn't call a six-pack but more a toast rack.

GERRY FARRELL (Airdrie): Big time 'Charlie' Stevie McCormick turned up at Airdrie with the reputation as a goalscorer and left with a reputation as a corner flag. He had so many holocausts playing for us we nicknamed him "Chernobyl" – and it stuck.

STEPHEN SWIFT: Craig Higgins once phoned Neil Watt at Stranraer to say that he couldn't turn up for training because he had really bad hay fever – in October. He insists it affects him badly.

STEVIE MURRAY: I'd like to add another foot as I am only 5ft 4in. I think maybe only Brian McLaughlin was smaller than me. I don't think it has been a disadvantage for me and it sometimes works well to have a low centre of gravity. Mark Roberts would call me 'The Human Crumb' and told me I need a high chair. But he could do with his forehead coming down a bit, while Gary Harkins could do with a face transplant. He's not a pretty boy.

DEREK MCINNES: Barry Robson. He is the spitting image of Charlie Dimmock from *Ground Force*.

PAUL HARTLEY (St Johnstone, Hibs, Hearts, Celtic, Scotland): Keigan Parker is Eddie Large, no doubt about it. One of the boys told me that he was out in town ripping up £20 notes. He just thinks he's it. He's massive – at least he thinks he is. He got a brand new MG with a reggie plate which said KEIGAN. It was scratched a few times and he kept wondering why. The boy is up there on his own when it comes to cockiness.

DENNIS NEWALL (East Stirling): Gordon Parks, the ex-Clyde player, played for me at Lesmahagow. I was going to pick him up for a game but from the look in his eyes it appeared as if he had been drinking the night before. He said: "No gaffer, it's the shampoo I've been using." To this day and four years later I still can't find that shampoo he was talking about.

PAUL LOVERING: Ian McCall called me 'Tripod' – for obvious reasons! Ian and Kenny Brannigan also called me 'The Bin Man' because they said if it wasn't for my dad I'd be working the bins. The Clydebank fans used to call me 'The Fish' because when I jumped up and down my mouth opened all the time.

KEVIN FOTHERINGHAM (Arbroath, Brechin, Forfar, East Fife): The funniest thing I've seen is John Potter trying to clear a ball with his left foot. He is so one-footed. At Clyde we would call his boots his Puma Standfinders.

KEVIN GALLACHER (Scotland Hall of Famer): At Blackburn, we would sit and have meals and Chris Sutton and Billy McKinlay would leave the table and come back with beanie hats looking like Rastafarians. They would then chuck potatoes and pasta at people.

MICHAEL MOORE (Stranraer, Hamilton, St Johnstone): Scott Struthers tried to get me to dance with him in a cage at Hamilton Palace nightclub. I'm not much of a dancer so I just watched him shaking his stuff.

CRAIG MCEWAN (Raith, Brechin): Paul Lovering always brags about how big his privates are and is quite within his rights. He would swagger about the dressing room telling the boys to take a look – John Hughes would grab them and drag him across the dressing room by them.

MICKY WEIR: Gordon Hunter is the only ginger guy I know who could pull the birds. The boy had talent.

ALAN ROUGH (Scotland keeper and Real Radio presenter): I have been kidding on our website that Ewen Cameron has got three nipples. People actually believe Ewen has got three nipples and pull him up about it so he is finding it a little hard to deal with.

GREG SHIELDS: I know Brian Reid from my time at Rangers and also Dunfermline. There was a well-known Glasgow transvestite called Shabbaz who would go to Bennets gay bar and was rumoured to fancy Brian. But he didn't take it well when he was slagged about it. We would pin things up in the dressing room about it.

DARREN MACKIE (Aberdeen): We would call Ryan Esson 'Frank the Tank' from the film *Old School* because he has got two personalities. He was so loud and hyper when he came into training. He must take happy pills.

MARTYN CORRIGAN: David Clarkson has a sock fetish. He was forever sitting in the corner of the Motherwell dressing room throwing socks at people while they were reading the paper or getting ready. Other boys tried it and got hit with a £10 fine, but David never got caught, even though he was the main culprit.

SCOTT MCCULLOCH: We caught our captain Marc Smyth shaving his chest hair. We found out about it because he didn't do a very good job of it. I think he thinks it makes him a bit more aerodynamic. It certainly raised a few eyebrows in the dressing room.

RYAN MCGUFFIE: We were at Stirling services and I used one of the phones to send a text to Davie Irons pretending to be his ex-wife's partner and the message said: "What are you doing showing your face around here? Get out of here!" We were killing ourselves laughing when Davie started looking around for him. He was raging.

GRAHAM BAYNE: Stuart McCaffrey's golf swing is the funniest thing I've seen. Even though he plays off five, he is like an old man. His swing is ridiculous and he takes forever. Caff mysteriously seems to get a good lie in the rough though.

BRYAN PRUNTY: Stephen McKeown says Kevin Christie looks like Shrek while Graham Holmes would call Paul Lovering 'Tomato Face'.

LIAM BUCHANAN: I wouldn't mind being a few inches taller as I am only 5ft 7in. Mark Baxter could do with an a**e reduction as it's huge. We could change Gary Fusco's hair colour as he is ginger. He tries to hide it with blond bits but it isn't happening. He tries to pass himself off as a strawberry blond.

ALAN GOW: Martin Glancy slagged me saying that my face was the strangest thing he has seen. That was rich coming from him when he looks like Robert the Bruce's dad in *Braveheart*. I speak to Martin all the time. He once owned a taxi and ran out of petrol while he had a passenger in the back. How stupid is that?

SIMON MENSING: Jack Ross used to call me 'Sloth' from *The Goonies*. We called him 'Federico' from *Big Brother* because he is his spitting image. He hates that. I'm also called 'Gunther' from *Friends*. Peter MacDonald was called 'David West' because he is the spitting image in every way.

PAUL MATHERS: After a 4-0 Dundee derby defeat, the chairman Malcolm Reid took exception to Billy Dodds who had been sent off in that game. Billy threw a sports drink bottle on to the ground and it bounced up and hit Malcolm on his nose, knocking his glasses off. They went for each other and it took four guys to prise them apart. Malcolm is an ex-ice hockey player and once he appeared to calm down, he went after Billy again after telling me to look after his glasses.

PAUL MCHALE: At Clyde, Neil McGregor was known as 'Sally Webster' from *Coronation Street* because of his blond hair-do.

JIM PATERSON: The taxi drivers in Dundee used to call Charlie Miller 'Spiderman' because every time he came out of a pub or club, he was always clinging to the walls. Charlie is a great bloke and we had a few good nights out together along with Paul Gallacher.

DAVID ELEBERT: The lads keep telling me how Scott Struthers likes to get up and dance at the Hamilton Palace nightclub. One day, Scott's phone went off and the ringtone was Christina Aguilera's song 'Candyman'. I have no idea why he had it and maybe he should explain that to everyone.

CRAIG SAMSON: Kris Boyd is into Cyndi Lauper. Honestly, he would listen to her all the time when he was at Kilmarnock.

MARK CAMPBELL: At Ayr United, we had a schoolboys and schoolgirls theme. Basically, half the squad had to dress up as boys and the other half as girls. Luckily for me, I was a boy. But guys such as Paul Lovering and Eddie Annand were the girls. They had to wear knee length socks and make up. Paul isn't the best-looking bloke and he makes an even worse woman. I think he enjoyed putting the make-up on, though. They were really into it.

SCOTT CHAPLAIN: Stevie Murray shops in the Bear Factory so he can get clothes to fit him.

MIKE FRASER: Rory McAllister would get called 'Dolph' after the actor Dolph Lundgren, who played Ivan Drago in *Rocky IV* because they have the same jawline. Lewis MacKinnon, who is now at Buckie Thistle gets called 'Chandon' because of his love of the high life. I get called 'Eike' because I am told I am spitting image of the German keeper Eike Immel, who played for Manchester City. I get called that more than my real name.

TOM PARRATT (American at Hamilton): I got slagged off for my bottom lip by David Elebert and was called 'Bubba' but he could do with a big tub of Just For Men hair colour since he is grey all over. He tried to claim he looks like George Clooney. That doesn't wash. Alex Neil got called 'Alex Reid' because he was the son the manager never had. David Winters was known as 'Turkey Touch' for obvious reasons while I would sometimes get called "that Yankee B*****d!" Brian Easton was known as the 'Human Head' and James McArthur was 'The Rat'.

JIM BALLANTYNE: My sister Anne and I fight like a cat and dog and have done since we were kids. I once threw a tin of mushrooms at her when I was about eight and she ended up stabbing a pencil through my eyelid – I still have the scar. When people see us argue they run a mile.

CHRIS SWAILES: James McArthur and Brian Easton – they are pretty cocky. They are lovely lads but they are gobsh**es!

RYAN MCCANN: Craig McKeown knows all the *Dirty Dancing* moves. Sorry friend, but you shouldn't know those moves. Neil McGregor is absolutely chronic – he just freezes on the dance floor. Paul Burns is the spitting image of Mr Burns from *The Simpsons*. I mean, they even have the same name.

DAVID PROCTOR: Rory McAllister is terrified of spiders. We found one in the changing room and put it inside his hair-wax tub so when he saw it he ended up screaming like a girl and ran out the changing room.

STEPHEN DOBBIE (Queen of the South, Swansea, Blackpool): Neil MacFarlane is called 'Homer Simpson' – I don't think I need to explain that one. Wee Stevie Murray is known as 'Danny DeVito'. I think Ian McCall is the spitting image of Jack Osbourne. At St Johnstone, Steven Anderson got called 'Sloth' from *The Goonies* and Gerry McCabe was known as 'Gene Wilder'.

MARC TWADDLE: I get slagged off about my nose so I would change that. Scott Chaplain could do with surgery to remove his saggy breasts. His body looks like that of an eighty-year-old.

BRIAN WAKE: Iain 'Beany' Russell is a tranny in the making. Feminine is not the word! He would spend ages on his blonde tinted hair and when he got tackled in training he yelped like a big girl.

GARY MCDONALD: We used to call Garry Hay 'Chicken Legs' because he has got the skinniest legs in the world. He needs to beef them up a bit as they are like women's legs.

CRAIG BRYSON (Kilmarnock): Gary Locke used to call Mehdi Taouil 'Pingping' after the smallest guy in the world because he's his spitting image. Mehdi didn't like it and because Pingping died recently, it has started again. Mehdi isn't happy.

GARY HARKINS: I would make Ian Maxwell's head smaller because it takes up too much space in the dressing room. I would give Scott Chaplain a boob job because his are sagging quite a bit. I would probably make Kevin McKinley less camp as there would be serious question marks over him if he wasn't married. I would also make David Rowson less creepy. You actually get shivers when he smiles at you and it is very disturbing.

CRAIG MCKEOWN: Stevie Masterton and an un-named Rangers player both pulled on a night out and they took them back to Stevie's mum's house. They switched girls and we all got word of this, as did Joe Miller. Joe pulled Stevie in and said the papers had got hold of the story and the girls were even rating both players out of ten. Stevie couldn't believe it, phoned his mum in shame and told her what had happened before Joe told him it was a wind-up. It was brilliant.

Doh!

EVER felt like the ground would just swallow you up? Footballers do all the time and no wonder when they have a brain the size of a peanut!

CRAIG MCEWAN: One time I was driving Paul Lovering, Neil Scally and James Grady and they kept annoying me by invading my driving space. I told Lovers if he touched me again I'd chuck him out the car. He did, so I pulled over and got out to drag him out but he locked the car, slid on to the driver's seat and drove off.

BRYAN GILFILLAN (Cowdenbeath, Gretna, Peterhead): I was driving back from training with Gretna when I decided to cut in on a line of cars as we approached a roundabout. Everyone started honking their horns, shouting abuse and giving me the finger. I couldn't understand why – until it clicked that I had just jumped a funeral procession.

MARTYN CORRIGAN: I was training on my own when I noticed a group of people at the other end of the pitch. I was running to and from the eighteen-yard boxes when I saw them throwing something in the air. I shouted at them and then I choked on a cloud of dust. It was a funeral party throwing ashes on to the pitch and I ended up swallowing half of them.

CHRIS JARDINE: I was at a birthday party for Gary and Ross Kerr and they invited my mates Gaz and Moff. But they were the only ones who thought it was a fancy dress party and Gaz turned up as a gorilla with Moff beside him as John Travolta.

ROBERT SNODGRASS: I did an April Fool on 31 March by mistake. I texted my girlfriend and one of the lads at Livingston, Gary Miller, saying I'd been fighting and had my nose burst open. She phoned me straight away to tell me I was a day early. She was raging I'd made her panic but then she was laughing when she realised how badly I'd messed it up.

CRAIG LEVEIN (Scotland manager): We were playing Dundee United and near the end of the match the referee blew his whistle. I shook hands with Eamonn Bannon before heading up the tunnel. But I found it very strange that I could only hear the sound of my own studs. I then looked round to see the game was still raging. The referee had only blown for a throw-in. I sneaked back on the pitch but as soon as I did he blew up for real.

ALAN GOW: Boxer Gary McArthur is a friend of mine and we visited a pal, who has a Jacuzzi and a plasma TV in the bathroom. We decided to run the Jacuzzi so we could relax in it and watch the big telly. However, we ended up putting bubble bath in it, which you aren't supposed to do, and the whole bathroom filled up with bubbles. We ended up trying to push the bubbles down the toilet and the whole place was soaking wet. It was Gary who put the bubble bath in and I started up the machine.

ANDY TOD: My outside light wasn't working so I phoned the club sparky Kenny Arnott to see if he could have a look at it. I thought the bulb might have gone. But after a while looking at it, he flicked on a switch I hadn't noticed. The light came on. I thought it was one of those that came on when you walked past. I felt really stupid.

TONY FITZPATRICK (St Mirren legend): We were having a pre-match meal on our way to Tannadice when one of the jokers in the pack, Lex Richardson, started mucking around with a sgian dubh at the table. Alex Beckett was telling him to chuck it because he was annoying him. Lex continued to mess around with it and even pretended to stab him – only he did actually stab him. Alex was wearing a white shirt and there was blood all over it. It is funny looking back on it.

STEVE LOVELL: For weeks I was telling everyone how excited I was about getting a Noble M12 GT03, how there are only so many being made and how it does 0-60 in next to no time. When

I went to collect it the rain was teeming down. The guy from the showroom handed me the keys and told me to have fun but just twenty minutes later I tried to overtake someone, slid across the road, spun 360 degrees and wound up in a ditch. It took me six months to get the car back.

DAVIE IRONS: I was playing for Ayr when the physio held up the No.10 board. Thinking it was me, I ran off, shook hands with the sub and was about to head off up the tunnel when someone shouted: "Irons you numpty, you are wearing No.6."

SCOTT STRUTHERS: When we were coming back from Montrose with the Third Division trophy in 2001, I was convinced I'd lost the lid. I had this awful feeling that it had been chucked out with the rubbish when we had a pit stop at McDonald's in Dundee on the way home. I had the celebrations interrupted and the bus turned upside down until I remembered I'd already hidden it in case it got lost.

JOHN MCVEIGH: One funny moment at the coaching course at Inverclyde was when we tried to turn a drunk Brian Aherne over on his bed but he fell down the other side. He cracked his head open and had blood pouring down when he stood up. We were all laughing even though it was quite serious.

DAVID WINNIE (St Mirren, Aberdeen): I was assistant manager at KR Reykjavik and while we were losing 3-0, I started ranting and raving at the team. I kicked a water bottle that was lying on the floor and it ricocheted off a bag and hit the manager Peter Petersson in the groin. I was half way through my rant so I couldn't stop but I could see the players were biting their lips, trying not to laugh. I was so embarrassed. Peter actually resigned the next day because we had started the season so badly.

CRAIG HINCHCLIFFE: I went with four of my mates to the World Cup in France in 1998. I told the lads I could speak French and get by in it. I got us to the place we were staying in by taxi but when we went to a restaurant and I looked at the menu, I couldn't understand anything. I couldn't make out to the rest of the guys I didn't understand it so I tried to bluff my way through. I thought the steak tartare looked nice. I never realised it was raw steak and I got a shock when it arrived. I took several bites before I excused myself and was sick in the toilet.

JOHN MCCORMACK (Ex-Dundee and Morton manager): The lads came in the dressing room after a very poor half and I said: "If you don't fancy it, I have three fresh legs on the bench to come on." Jim Duffy was in the corner killing himself with laughter and even I started chuckling when I realised how daft I'd been.

BRIAN MCPHEE (Airdrie, Livingston and Fireman): I hadn't quite mastered the use of Ralgex and thought you could spray it anywhere to ease the pain. I had a really bad groin strain so I reckoned I could put some Ralgex on and it would be fine. I sprayed the can in my pants, ran out for a warm-up and this unbelievable pain shot right up me. Needless to say that part of my anatomy was out of action for a while.

STEVIE TOSH: I was playing for Arbroath against Ross County in their first season in the league. I scored a hat-trick and then proceeded to tell the press that a few of the players had a bet on Arbroath to win. The club got their knuckles rapped off the SFA for gambling and I wasn't popular for letting the cat out of the bag.

STEVEN BOYACK (Rangers, Hearts, Livingston): I made a right fool of myself playing for Rangers youths. I was playing wide on the right and Billy Kirkwood shouted: "Tuck in Steven." I thought he was talking about my shirt and I stopped in the middle of the game to fix my appearance. He gave me pelters and said: "No you idiot, move into the middle."

PAUL KINNAIRD: The best prank I've been involved in was the famous incident involving John Lambie at Blackpool. I was the instigator who decided to get the boys together after beach training one day and throw the boss in the sea. Unfortunately, one of the lads dropped him and he ended up puncturing a lung. He was out of the game for six weeks – and gave me double training sessions for weeks afterwards when he returned as punishment.

CRAIG BREWSTER: My club car at Hibs had a dodgy handbrake so I always had to leave it in gear. Once, I was visiting a friend of mine, Ian Little, and parked on his steep driveway. When I went to leave, I was chatting to Ian and leaned into the car to start the engine, forgetting it was in gear. It jumped and started to roll down the driveway with me chasing after it. It ended up rolling across the street and smashing into the side of a neighbour's house. I was so embarrassed because it cost thousands of pounds of damage. The house belonged to an old couple and they must have thought the roof was caving in.

JAMIE MCALLISTER (Hearts, Aberdeen): I was out with my mates on a Sunday down the Plaza in East Kilbride and I walked smack into a plate glass door and battered my nose in front of a thousand shoppers.

JIM DUFFY: I was at the late Norrie McCathie's testimonial dinner and for a laugh, I pulled someone's chair away from them as they were sitting down. As they fell over Craig Levein's jacket got covered in red wine. I offered to pay the dry cleaning bill, but he said that wasn't good enough. I stood up and was toe-to-toe with him, my face about an inch away from his, and said: "Are you winding me up?" Craig said: "Yip!" I then replied: "Well you're lucky because I don't usually ask that question." He was half a second away from getting a Glasgow Kiss but was so cool it was the best wind-up ever.

RAY FARNINGHAM: During the wedding service when I was marrying Poppy, I was kneeling at the church and the price tag was still on my new platform shoes. The sticker read £2.50 – and the whole congregation saw it.

DARREN SHERIDAN: I was sitting in the dugout about to come off the bench in a game. Chris Armstrong scored and I jumped up to celebrate and hit my head against the roof. I cut my head and next thing I knew I was getting treatment in the dressing room.

MICHAEL MOORE: The daftest thing I have ever done is tell Billy McLaren to "f*** off" just before half time. When we got into the dressing room he pinned me up against the wall by the neck. It was pretty frightening. But he still sent me out for the second half. He is the hardest man I know.

SCOTT TUNBRIDGE (Hamilton): On my twenty-first birthday, I was doing athletics and competing in the long jump. Everyone else was going further than me so my dad took me to one side and tried to give me words of encouragement, telling me to jump like Superman. I went to jump and stuck my arm out like Superman and fell flat on my face into the sand – everyone else just p****d themselves laughing.

NEIL BARRETT (Dundee, Livingston): During a youth game for Chelsea against Liverpool, we got battered 1–0 and Jim Duffy was having a real go at the players. He got to Mark Royle and he told him: "You need to be more aggressive, like a ..." but he couldn't think of a word. He ended up blurting "ant". It was a situation where you couldn't laugh because he was so angry but then the physio laughed and then everyone was in stitches.

SCOTT MCCULLOCH: Brechin were about to play Falkirk when Dick Campbell, who is terrible with names and hasn't got the best handwriting, was giving us his team talk. He was telling us to watch out for a player called Hushey. We didn't have a clue what he was on about. It turned out he meant John Hughes and got the spelling of his name wrong.

STEVIE MILNE: I was in the Dundee youth team and one day I decided to take the minibus out of the main gate and drive it around. But I couldn't drive and I wedged the bus against the wall. I tried for ten minutes to get it out but couldn't and had to tell John McCormack, who wasn't too pleased. It took fifteen YTS boys and four coaching staff, including Cowboy, to lift the bus away from the wall. Luckily, I didn't have to pay for the damage.

JIM MCALISTER (Morton, Hamilton): About seven or eight years ago, my mates and I thought it would be good to go fishing in a polystyrene boat with only one oar. We ended up drifting and it got to the stage where we almost called the coastguard to rescue us as we were panicking so much, but we somehow managed to get back safely under own steam.

COLIN STEWART: At Ross County, the boys moved Steven McGarry's car and stuck grass all over it. In revenge, the same thing happened to David Winters' car. But there were stones amongst the grass and when David went to clear it, he scratched the roof of his car and it cost £900 to repair.

FRANK MCAVENNIE: I was drinking with Georgie Best one time and going on about how I'd been with two Miss UK's. George simply said: "Come back when you've been with four Miss Worlds." I never even reached one.

DUNCAN SHEARER: Scotland were playing the Faroes, but John Robertson, Andy Goram, Ally McCoist and I were all injured and we went for an Italian in Ayr. We were allowed some wine, but that turned into bottles with Andy. I forgot where my hotel room was when I came back steaming at 2am. I chapped on the door looking for my roommate Colin Calderwood, but Craig Brown answered half naked and wrapped with a towel. I was wondering what he was doing in my room. He just said: "Duncan, you're in the room below."

GRAHAM BAYNE: Zander Sutherland came up with a cracker when he thought the Netherlands was somewhere near Argentina. He didn't know it is actually Holland. His geography obviously isn't that great and he also asked if Dunfermline was close to Kilmarnock.

JOHN BURRIDGE: At Wolves, we had a weightlifting bar fixed in the dressing room so you could do chin-ups, but there was a live cable touching it. I went up to do my chins and got electrocuted. It was the best warm-up I could have.

PAUL MATHERS: You just wouldn't mess with Noel Blake who was at Dundee. He is 6ft 3in and looks like Mike Tyson and Frank

Bruno rolled into one. Gary McKeown once upset him by nailing his flip-flops to the floor – but they were given to Noel by his late grandmother. Noel was raging and Gary didn't own up until four years later – when he was in Japan.

TONY FITZPATRICK: When I was manager at St Mirren, we were drawing with Ayr in a cup tie and I was angry at half time. Things got quite heated and I smashed my fist on the massage table. I ended up dislocating three of my knuckles. I winced – but tried to keep it hidden from the players. I went into the bathroom to get the doctor to see to it. I cried like a baby.

GEORGE MCCLUSKEY: I once ordered a sweet after dinner and Jock Stein was raging. He didn't like us eating sweets. When Johnny Doyle arrived at the club, I told him it was fine to get a sweet. He ordered a massive Knickerbocker Glory. When Jock saw it he slammed it down and it went flying everywhere. Johnny was ready to kill me.

DAVE BAIKIE: When I was boss of Arbroath, I was ranting and raving at the players in the dressing room at half time. I shouted at them: "You're playing like ants round a queen bee." I didn't realise I had said it at the time but no one dared to laugh.

KEVIN RUTKIEWICZ (Aberdeen, St Johnstone): At Aberdeen, we were playing Dunfermline at East End Park and I was warming up behind the goal. An Aberdeen fan shouted at me for an autograph. When I turned round I clattered into the post that was holding the net up. I got a cut eye and the fans went crazy every time I warmed up. The police told me to sit on the bench as I was getting them too excited.

SCOTT CHAPLAIN: It was funny and strange seeing Ian McCall with foam all over his head but not realising it. He was slaughtering Ryan McStay so he took Ian's hat off and sprayed foam over his head. The gaffer never realised until he put his hat back on. He took it in good spirits though.

ALEX RAE: When I was at Falkirk, we went on a team bonding exercise to Aviemore. It was November and freezing at the time. We were going to do some white water rafting but before we did it I jumped into the water from a tree for a £10 each from the players. I didn't realise the rafting was for an hour so I was freezing the whole time. I had to sit at the front and kept getting soaked.

DYLAN KERR: Leeds United had just won the league and we went to Marbella at the end of the season. I pulled this cracking bird who was drop-dead gorgeous. When the girl left she left a note saying what a great night she had. Later that night I found a card under my door from the girl saying I was the most amazing thing she ever had and I was an Adonis in bed. I showed everyone, including Gordon Strachan, telling them to read it and weep. On the flight home, the pilot announced for me to come to the cockpit. I went up and there were all the players laughing – they'd written the card. I felt like such a p***k.

DEAN HOLDEN (Falkirk): We were in New York on holiday walking around Central Park when I suddenly realised we had overstayed by a day. I got my times and dates mixed up and we should have left the day before. We went to the airport and had to shell out a few hundred quid to get a flight back.

GORDON SMITH (Former SFA Chief Executive): When I moved to Brighton in 1980 I got a phone call from a Mr Brighton who said he wanted to buy my house. I thought it was one of the lads at Rangers like Peter McCloy playing a wind-up. I wasn't very polite and was sarcastically saying: "Yeah, yeah, come on over tomorrow night." But he actually did exist and he did turn up at the house wearing a trilby hat. He bought my house. I had to apologise.

DAVID RAE: I took this girl to the pictures but my old Austin car wouldn't start because the battery was flat so I would always leave it on a hill so I could bump-start it. But when I was taking the girl home it didn't start and I had to get her to help me push my car back up the hill to try and start it again. It was our first date and no surprise, she didn't go back out with me. We bump into each other from time to time and she always reminds me.

DAVID PROCTOR: Russell Duncan is the worst minibus driver. He tried to accelerate over a speed bump but I came flying off my seat and into the air. I smacked my eye off the seat belt holder and the gaffer thought I'd been fighting after he saw the state of my face.

CHRIS JARDINE: I once went into a shop and asked how much the two-pence banana sweeties were.

DON HUTCHISON: I took a girl out on a date when I was at West Ham and went to the bar and asked for two Scotch on the rocks ... without ice. The bird gave me a strange look. When I left West Ham the lads wrote it down on a shirt for me.

ADAM COAKLEY: I was cleaning my car and trying to get in behind the automatic gearbox. But I slipped it into drive and ended up crashing through my garage door. The door was all smashed and the car was scraped. I have had a few crashes. I wrote off my first car after two weeks. I went round a corner too fast, skidded and clipped a tree.

PAT STANTON (Hibs legend): I was playing for Hibs against Falkirk at Brockville when there was a lull in the play. A guy leaned over the barrier, so I said hello to him, but he said: "I've never really liked you." I asked him if he came to watch Falkirk often and he replied: "Why would I do that? I'm a Hibs fan." The woman next to him simply said: "Well, you did ask."

KEVIN MCDONALD: I fell for the classic cream cake prank when I was on loan at Airdrie. All the lads had a sniff at the fresh cream saying it was off and there was only one place the cake ended up ... on my face.

MATT ELLIOTT (Scotland): I went to Oxford to have signing talks and headed right into reception. I told the girl there I was Matt Elliott and there for signing talks, but she looked at me with a completely blank expression on her face. It turned out I was at the local dog track and Oxford's stadium was further down the road.

BRIAN MARTIN: Motherwell played Hibs at Easter Road and wee Kevin Harper ran through on goal to score and make it 2–0. I looked at the linesman because I thought he was offside and made a gesture to him that he had a bit of a belly. The linesman told the referee who then sent me off. The linesman had also heard me calling him a fat b*****d. I thought he hadn't heard that.

MAX RUSHDEN (*Soccer AM* presenter): Our guest Trevor Nelson said he had lost Stevie Wonder's number, so I said: "Stevie, if you are watching, give us a call!" Enough said.

CRAIG BRYSON: I ordered my private reg plate from the DVLA website. They only send you a bit of paper so you can get the plates yourself but I didn't realise that and phoned them up asking why they hadn't been delivered to my door. I told the boys in the dressing room and I got a bit of stick for it.

8

Fashion Disasters

FOOTBALLERS are renowned for their impeccable dress sense – Armani, Gucci, Hugo Boss – but then there are a select few who wouldn't know decent clobber staring them in the face. Here are the verdicts on the fashion in the dressing rooms ...

STEWART EASTON (Stenhousemuir): Mark Wilson had this Italian theme going on because he's swarthy with the stubble and the jet-black hair. But he's not so much Armani as Man at C&A – and even then he spoiled the whole look by coming into training still wearing his ID badge from his job at the gas board call centre.

CHRIS MILLAR: Andy McLaren was on the treatment table and he whipped down his shorts to reveal a sparkly purple thong! Douglas Rae walked in and Andy said: "What do you think of these Mr Chairman?" He didn't know where to look.

JIM LAUCHLAN: When I was at Kilmarnock, Alex Totten had a policy of no denim or you'd be fined. The day after he announced it, Craig Napier came in wearing a suit. He was wearing three-quarter-length trousers, pink spray-painted shoes, a pink shirt, a pink tie, a suit jacket with the sleeves too wee for him and his shirt sleeves too big. He completed the look with a pair of shades.

PAUL BURNS (Queen of the South): Neil Scally nicked Martyn Lancaster's digital camera. Scally went through it and found snaps of Martyn posing with a red thong on. Scally made copies and posted them all over the walls of the ground.

JIM PATERSON: A few of us went to a nightclub for a Christmas night out and we had all decided to wear Hawaiian shirts. We went in but didn't realise the bouncer thought we were gay and told us to go through the door that led to the gay section of the club. I didn't catch on until I was in the toilets and a man tried to pick me up by commenting on the size of my privates. The four of us left and had a go at the bouncer. He said: "What was I supposed to think with you dressed like that?"

KEVIN RUTKIEWICZ: I dressed as Captain Jack Sparrow from *Pirates of the Caribbean* at Halloween. But because I had been out all night, I didn't have time to get changed. So I came into training on the Monday morning dressed up as the Captain. I changed into my gear but still had the black nail polish and black eye-liner on. Owen Coyle wanted to see me afterwards but because I didn't have a change of clothes I went in to see him with my costume still on. He told me to f*** off and get out!

ALLAN PRESTON: At St Johnstone, we had a night out in Edinburgh and decided to have a '70s theme. Roddy Grant dressed up as Björn from ABBA, complete with blonde wig. We accidentally wandered into a gay bar and as we were leaving some guy outside called Roddy a poof and then punched him, breaking his jaw. When the rest of us came out all we saw was this wig lying on the floor.

STEVE BOWEY: David Bagan in his underpants is the worst thing I have ever seen. The boy doesn't own any boxers – just these awful navy blue and grey pants.

ALLAN PRESTON: I would call David McNamee 'Vincent van Gogh' because he has part of his ear missing. He looks like he dresses in the dark – plus I think he likes to wear women's clothes.

JOHN HUGHES: I once dressed up as a *Playboy* bunny girl to try and win a scooter in a fancy dress competition. I was seventeen. I had the fishnets, the bunny tail and the bunny ears on but I didn't win.

STEPHEN CRAIGAN (Partick, Motherwell): James 'Banjo' McKinstrey would come in with green, white and orange Dunlop trainers, old club trackie bottoms, an un-ironed pink t-shirt and a Celtic boys' club trackie top.

HARRY CAIRNEY (Brechin, Annan): I had a tartan shirt and trousers along with platform shoes, which I wore in the '70s at the time of the Bay City Rollers. There is actually a picture of me wearing the outfit with Billy McNeill. It is horrific.

JOHN MAISANO (Morton): I have a blue g-string and a pair of leather trousers which I used to wear. I still have them back home in Melbourne. I don't think it would be a good idea if I wore them to the James Watt pub in Greenock.

BRIAN MCGINTY (St Mirren): I had an Issey Miyake white shirt which buttoned up the side and looked more like a dentist's shirt! I also had a bright orange Versace shirt and a pair of red jeans, which didn't go together – I was going through a phase of wearing bright things.

KEVIN DRINKELL (Rangers, Falkirk): When Davie Dodds came to have signing talks with Rangers at a hotel, he wore jeans and borrowed the hotel porter's suit so he would look smart. Of course, some of the boys like Ian Durrant got wind of it and destroyed the suit. I got the backlash when the hotel porter's wife spotted me in the town and had a go at me.

DAVIE NICHOLLS: Graeme Connell has worn women's underwear before. We had a party once and he lost a bet so had to put on a g-string and ask the milkman for a pint of milk. He came back with the milk and a smile on his face. He didn't seem embarrassed, in fact, I'm sure he wears g-strings all the time now.

DICK CAMPBELL (Dunfermline, Brechin, Forfar): I scored against Alan Rough in 1976 and went mental running behind the goals to celebrate. I ran so far that people had to stop me saying I'd be out the ground if I kept going. But that wasn't embarrassing – my beard at the time was. You'd do anything in those days, so big Jim Leishman and I both had Bee Gees-style beards. Times change don't they? Back then, Big Leish was a size 32 in trousers, now he's a 32 round the ankles.

GAVIN RAE: We wore dodgy gear on a Dundee Christmas night out like mismatching pink shirts and bright yellow trousers out of all the charity shops. I remember one year, Hugh Robertson turned up as the Pope, and others as Elvis, Robin Hood and Postman Pat.

CRAIG TAGGART (Stirling Albion): Eddie Cunnington used to insist on wearing tatty Gola trainers that he tried to trump up as Diesel ones. He sewed a 'D' on a pair he bought at the Barras. Franck Escalon had the worst collection of Christmas jumpers I've ever seen. I was sick of seeing his tops with snowflakes and snowmen. I thought French people had taste.

EDDIE ANNAND (Dundee, Ayr): James Grady's dress sense scares me. He came into training one week with some fake Nike trainers that looked suspiciously like woman's shoes. We later discovered they belonged to his missus Emma and he tried to worm his way out of it by saying they had the same size feet. It must be difficult for him to get proper gear though because he is so small.

Even some of the clobber my daughter Chloe wears would be too big for him.

SCOTT WALKER: When I first saw our French keeper Ludovic Roy I nearly killed myself laughing. He wore the most ridiculous white shoes you will ever see. They were long and pointed and look like bowling shoes – or something John Travolta might wear.

CRAIG THOMSON (Referee): Iain Brines once turned up at training wearing Superman underwear. He said his kids bought them for him but after the slagging he took he came back wearing them again. Charlie Richmond goes for the jumper-over-the-shoulders look. Someone needs to tell them both that Primark is not trendy.

ROBERT SNODGRASS: When I was at Livi, I didn't have a jacket so I wore my dad's to training one day. It was a wee jacket, like a grandpa jacket with patterns inside and I thought it went all right with what I'd had on. But when I came in after training, it had been cut up into about six or seven pieces. It was my dad's favourite jacket so I got a roll of Sellotape and tried to tape it back together. He just burst out laughing when he saw it.

ALLAN RUSSELL (Hamilton, St Mirren, Kilmarnock): David Fernandez looks like he's getting ready to go to a gay convention half the time. He came in wearing a matching white shirt and three-quarter length trousers. It was horrendous.

MARTIN GLANCY (Airdrie): Willie Wilson at Airdrie dressed like Crockett from *Miami Vice* because he would wear the white suits and wouldn't wear any socks.

STEVEN CRAIG (Aberdeen, Motherwell, Ross County): At Motherwell, Scott McDonald had a couple of friends who looked like Starsky and Hutch in drag at a night out. Kevin Christie had a pair of jeans that were two inches too short, plus he had a golf bag that was so thin it looked like a pencil case. I did own a Valentino cardigan and when I saw a sixty-five-year-old man walk by with the same one on I stopped wearing it. My mum uses it as a duster now.

CRAIG NELSON (Falkirk, Ayr, Brechin, Hearts): We had a school night out. Half the players went as schoolboys and half as schoolgirls, including Neil Scally who looked like Sonia from *Eastenders*. At St Johnstone, Ian Maxwell dressed up as Mary Poppins even though it was a superhero theme, while Brian McLaughlin was Cat Woman but was more like Midget Man. Paul Lovering wore some good labels but it was like a bin man wearing Armani and Prada. It was funny seeing Brian McLaughlin dressed up in clothes from Baby Gap. I once paid £300 for a hideous Armani tartan bomber jacket, which my father-in-law now uses to clean out the rabbit hutch.

JERRY O'DRISCOLL: When I was out of the team at Dundee I thought I'd improve my chances of playing by having a moustache because Peter and Jimmy Marr, Jimmy Bone and Jocky Scott all had them. I looked like a German pimp and it never worked.

RICHIE FORAN (Motherwell, Caley Thistle): Gordon Marshall wore some ropey gear and dressed like he was in the '70s. David Cowan had a black pair of jeans with yellow stripes on the back of them. He must have worn them for a laugh, there is no way he could have actually liked them.

PAUL MCGRILLEN: George Burley used to come into Motherwell with jeans with Fred Flintstone on his thigh. He must have been about thirty-four at the time and they were just horrendous.

GREG STRONG (Motherwell): When I was just seventeen at Wigan, I had an electric blue suit jacket and I would wear it all the time. I got hammered for it though and when I walked in the players would laugh, march behind me and say, "Here comes the band."

JIMMY SANDISON (Hearts, Airdrie): My most memorable night out was a Hearts Christmas night out, where unfortunately I drew the short straw and had to wear the French maid's outfit. Trying to flag a taxi later on was eventful.

MICKY WEIR: At a Hibs Christmas night out, I ended up as Wee Willie Winkie, surprisingly enough. Alan Sneddon was dressed up as Superman – he disappeared and we didn't know where he was until he jumped out of a phone box pretending to fly. He kept doing it all along Princes Street and was pretty funny.

NEIL BARRETT: Derek Adams had got these big granddad y-fronts rather than a nice pair of fashionable Calvin Kleins.

KEVIN TINDAL: Mark McWalter at Arbroath once bought a pair of light blue suede slip-on shoes – because he got a pair of dark blue ones for free. Barry Sellars at Arbroath would go on every night out wearing the same blue shirt. He claimed he had different ones. He'd wear it fifteen times and claimed he had fifteen different shirts.

ALEX WILLIAMS: We had to pick names from a hat for a Christmas night out with Morton and then provide them with a £10 outfit. I got Stewart Greacen and bought him a chef's outfit with multi-coloured trousers and a hat. We ended up pouring pints over each other's heads.

CHRIS MILLAR: There was a kid at Morton called Gary Loughran who we nicknamed 'Horrible Hair'. His hair was shaved, with tramlines on the back and ginger spikes. It was terrible. I admit I've had a couple of dodgy ones – but that's because there was girl I liked in a hairdressers and I said she could do my hair so I could speak to her. It was a disaster. She dyed it red and I had to shave it all off. But I went out with her for a bit so it was worth it.

RYAN MCGUFFIE: I bought a black leather jacket for £200 which I got a caning for but I think that is my best item of clothing. I'm just misunderstood. They just didn't appreciate it and called me 'The Fonz'. John O'Neil has some dodgy brown sandals, Stevie Tosh looks like he has been dragged through a bush backwards and James Grady's clothes hang off him. As for Kenny Deuchar, well, he dresses like a doctor.

STEVIE MILNE: I had a white Gucci shirt which I bought for about £70 but as soon as I showed it to my wife Leeanne, she said it looked like a woman's blouse so I put it in the bin. Martin Hardie is the worst-dressed at St Johnstone: the boy slags me off about my gear but he needs to look in a mirror. Nothing he wears goes.

FRANK MCAVENNIE: I used to wear a lot of leather gear and I'd a cream suit which made me look like Don Johnson in *Miami Vice*. Charlie Nicholas would buy the designer stuff while I used to buy the labels and sew them on.

DANNY CUNNING (Livingston and Hamilton kit-man): The lad Gus Bahoken was the worst dressed at Livi. I remember he was in Princes Street one day with about five shopping bags. He was arrested by police because they thought he'd stolen them. He could hardly speak any English and phoned the club to get us to explain to them. Robert Snodgrass had an awful satin tracksuit jacket. I used to own a tartan jacket á la Rod Stewart.

BRYAN GILFILLAN: Steve Paterson once wore his Bob the Builder outfit to training at Caley Thistle. We had our Christmas night out and everyone was the worse for wear the next morning. Steve didn't have a change of clothes with him so he walked in the next day with the full outfit on.

ROY AITKEN (Former Celtic captain): Pat Bonner once came in with this horrendous coat on to training. It was so bad, we hung it from the flagpole right above the old Jungle.

MARK MCGHEE: I would certainly change John McMaster's fashion sense. He was a real corduroy man and would have patches on his clothes.

FRANK MCGARVEY (St Mirren, Celtic): I bought a gold/yellow coloured suit but when I went on the team bus, Alex Ferguson said: "You look like a Bombay money lender." I didn't wear it ever again.

STEPHEN SIMMONS: Scott Wilson turned up at a black and white function boasting he bought a George shirt from Asda for £4. No wonder he has a big house because he doesn't spend any money on clothes.

JOHN MCMASTER: I was always a target for the fashion but Gordon Strachan had a few disasters as well though. He had this white anorak and he would always wear it but it had food stains all over it. If you gave big Alex McLeish any stick at all about his gear then he would just show you the label.

SIMON MENSING: Kevin Rutkiewicz has the best selection of briefs known to man. He has Marvel Comics underwear and Superman briefs. He also has red long johns.

WILLIE KINNIBURGH: At one point in any night out, it is guaranteed Scott Chaplain will be swinging his jumper around his head.

PAUL MATHERS: Robbie Raeside had this leather jacket for at least ten years. He was obviously getting his money's worth. Dean Keenan would wear his jeans halfway down his a**e so you see his boxer shorts.

JIM BETT (Rangers, Aberdeen): When Roy Aitken was No.2 to Willie Miller at Aberdeen, he had jumpers that matched the dye in his hair. He obviously wanted to conceal his greying hair. But when his hair looked the same colour as his green jumper, the boys ribbed him about it.

ANDY TOD: I have four double crowns and a coo's lick for hair. I actually want to have Tom Cruise's hair. My mate Mark and I tried to get a Tom Cruise cut when we were younger, after he'd starred in *Top Gun* – it looked more like Mr Majeika.

ALAN REID (Hibs, St Mirren): At Hibs, we had a lot of foreign players and you can imagine the different tastes in styles and fashion they had. Mathias Doumbe had some bad clothes, including a jumper that had seagulls on it! In the St Mirren dressing room, the lads played it safe with their styles, although I have to say Mark Corcoran had some clothes that can only be described as different. In particular, a red, leather-styled jacket that's straight from Michael Jackson's *Thriller* video.

GEORGE MCCLUSKEY: Davie Provan had these tight jeans and loved wearing four-inch heels because he wanted to look taller.

PAUL MCHALE: Craig McKeown's clothes are just plain offensive. He would wear ridiculous things and can't mix and match. He would come in at Clyde with brown shoes, green trackies and a purple t-shirt. Horrible!

JIM PATERSON: Stuart Duff was just a terrible dresser at Tannadice. He would wear drainpipe jeans. I bet you he still has them. I used to own a purple Versace shirt with VERSACE in huge letters on the back of it. I got pelters for that.

DAVID ELEBERT: We were planning to go out in Edinburgh at Christmas wearing fancy dress and we picked a colour theme. But because we ran out of colours we decided not to bother in the end and just dress as normal – only we didn't tell Alex Neil. He turned up wearing a polka dot costume! He even had red polka dot shoes and a polka dot headband.

MICHAEL GARDYNE: Neil Lennon once came into the dressing room at Parkhead wearing stonewashed jeans and a denim jacket and Craig Beattie just slaughtered him. But when Craig came back in after training later on and went to put his tracksuit on, Neil had cut holes at the knees and the elbows. Craig was absolutely raging about it at first but he eventually saw the funny side.

TRENT MCCLENAHAN (Hamilton): Hamilton went to Newcastle for a Christmas night out and there were quite a few drinks put away and some outrageous outfits. And some of them made some hot-looking women – James McArthur, James McCarthy, Mark McLaughlin, Brian Easton and Lucas-J Akins. They were all dolled up with skirts, make-up and wigs. Lucas actually got mistaken for a chick. There were some good costumes. Alex Neil went as Michael Jackson, David Elebert went as Edward Scissorhands and struggled to drink his pint.

KEVIN RUTKIEWICZ: Stephen Payne was warned if he put on his red Adidas bottoms there would be trouble. Sure enough, he wore them into training and they ended up on the Pittodrie flag pole. The pockets were stuffed with bread to attract the birds. When he got them back down they were covered in droppings.

MIKE FRASER: John Rankin got dressed up as a woman with heels and stockings for a Christmas night out. In fact, he came into training the day before wearing the costume.

JAMIE LANGFIELD: At Dundee, Dario Bonetti used to take training and, even worse, warm-ups before games in his big bubble jacket, camouflage cargo jeans and big boots, with a fag hanging out his mouth.

PAUL LAWSON (Celtic, Ross County): When we went to Magaluf, Craig Beattie turned up with these horrible sky blue shoes – they were so unbelievable we took pictures of them and then burnt them.

PAUL BURNS: With the type of clothes he wears, a lot of the boys are saying Craig Barr is a little too camp for his own good. I am sure he isn't but he does come in with thin scarves or multi-coloured pants and boxers.

FRANK GRAY (Leeds, Scotland): Jack Charlton used to come in with this leather jacket and the boys would rip into him for it. It was around the end of the Mods and Rockers era so some of the lads got elastoplasts and printed "Hell's Angels" on the back of his jacket.

RYAN MCCANN: Jim Thomson has these yellow Adidas trainers. I think he goes into his wardrobe every morning and tells himself he must wear the worst clothes possible. At his age, he also probably wears corduroys. I have a salmon – some would say pink – checked shirt, which I should have binned a long time ago but haven't.

STEPHEN DOBBIE: John 'Zippy' Henry was at St Johnstone with me and his gear was terrible. On 5 November when all the boys were away training, Peter MacDonald made a Guy out of cardboard boxes and stuck Zippy's gear on it – a light blue denim jacket and jeans with blue Adidas Gazelles. The boys were in stitches!

Hook, Line and Sinker

MAYBE I'm being harsh saying footballers are all thickos because it takes a genius to think up some of the following elaborate wind-ups. Absolute genius.

GREG STRONG: At Bolton, we played a trick on a lad called Mark Westhead. We were in the sauna but when myself and a guy called Stuart Whitehead came out, we took Mark's clothes and left just his car keys. We went to reception and asked for clothes from the lost property section and sent them up to Mark. He had no choice but to put on a crop top and a ten-year-old's tracksuit bottoms. He came down and I've never seen anyone run so fast to his car.

MICKY WEIR: Danny Lennon and I pulled a prank on the rest of the Hibs team at a German training camp. It was at the height of the IRA problems and people were on red alert. Danny had a relative in the army so he got us boots, camouflage jackets and balaclavas. We dressed up in the middle of the night and pre-tended we were in the IRA – complete with Irish accents. We got everyone out of their bunks and lined them up against a wall. I am telling you, grown men were crying. They never realised it was us. I remember that Steven Tweed was absolutely terrified and we had to take our masks off to convince him it wasn't for real. We won a bottle of champagne for that wind-up.

CRAIG HINCHCLIFFE: The boys at Airdrie played a cracker on Stevie Gray. It was the time when the Gulf War was just starting and we told Stevie it was only a matter of time before they called up footballers to fight. So we got a Ministry of Defence headed letter saying that he had been drafted in. The first paragraph was very professional, that he must report for duty. Then it went on to say if he'd any spare camouflage jackets to bring them along. It also asked if he had a second-hand tank!

MARC TWADDLE: There was a young lad called Harvey at Falkirk and when we were driving back from training Kieran McAnespie was mooning out of another car. Harvey stuck his head out the window to have a pop back. But the lads wound up the window so his head was stuck and he couldn't move. We were driving at 90mph with his head stuck out of the window.

DANNY CADAMARTERI: I had a running vendetta with Michael Ball at Everton and we went through a phase of destroying each other's clothes. When I was in the shower one time he decided to steal my training kit and all my clothes. He left me with just my car keys. I had to drive home totally naked. It would have been okay had it not been tea-time traffic.

DAVE BOWMAN (Dundee United): Christian Dailly was sixteen when he came on his first European trip with us to Iceland. We put some men's magazines in his socks. When he came back he gave his washing to his mum. We had to apologise to her.

DANNY GRAINGER: The lads at Dundee United made a crude number plate for Lee Wilkie's car. Lee got wind of this so he decided to fill everyone's pockets, socks and shoes with live crickets.

WILLIE KINNIBURGH: I got Craig Hinchcliffe a cracker. I swapped his car reg plate for my own home-made one which read "I BLOW DOGS". Craig was driving in Glasgow when he got stopped by the police and given three points.

ALLY GRAHAM (Man of many clubs): I was flush one week after an Albion Rovers win and decided to use my fiver win bonus to treat eight pals at the cinema. We all paid to see *Fatal Attraction* and I volunteered to buy the Cornettos. As soon as I left the hall to go buy them, everyone changed seats and I couldn't find them when I returned. The cinema was in hysterics. I just found a seat and shouted out: "I'll eat them all myself then." After five minutes, they shouted me over.

JOHN BURRIDGE: Bryan Robson was a guest on our TV show in Oman. The other pundit, Joe Morrison, told Bryan I'd forgotten to take my medication and I suffered from Tourette's syndrome. He told him that if I didn't take it, I could lose the plot live on TV. So we pretended the camera was rolling and I started shouting loud and twitching. Bryan was asked all about Barcelona and Chelsea and then Joe asked me what I thought, I just said: "Why don't you go and f*** off!" We showed it to Bryan later and he took it well, although he called us a "bunch of b*****ds!"

ZANDER DIAMOND: Darren Mackie and I used to go into the Pittodrie canteen and cut holes in the bottom of the polystyrene cups with a fork or scalpel, so when people went up for drinks they would spill through the hole. Sometimes people wouldn't realise their cup was dripping, and by the time they sat down, they had no juice left in their cup. I don't think anyone really knew it was us who did it.

GERRY COLLINS: John Lambie called the players "a shower of poofs" on TV and Tony Higgins wrote him a letter on pink paper pretending to be outraged and saying one of the Thistle directors was gay. John asked me: "Do you think any of them are poofs?" and told me he had always thought one of them looked like one before I told him it was a wind-up.

STEVE PATERSON: Someone – I suspect Duncan Shearer – crumbled black shoe polish into my socks. When I took them off to go to bed my feet were black – and they still are after a month as I can't get the dye out. Paul Cherry was a great practical joker and I remember he would go and buy a full outfit from Oxfam and wear it in the dressing room.

GERRY FARRELL: At Ross County, our coach Andy Dornan was always giving me a hard time. So four of us bought ski masks and while John Hewitt was talking to him on the park one day, we grabbed him, decked him and gave him a doing. He got soaked and picked up some bad bruises in a place I'd rather not mention. To this day he doesn't know who did it. I hope it still hurts, Andy!

CHRIS HILLCOAT: We got Gerry McCabe on a golfing outing. Willie McLean was the assistant at the time and he took us down to a club in Ayrshire. Gerry didn't have any clubs but George McCluskey told him not to worry, he would get him a set. He got him one but claimed there was no strap and he could only carry it by the handle. Little did Gerry know we put a couple of bricks in the bottom. By the time he finished the round he was knackered from carrying the bag and bricks. His right bicep was bulging.

STEPHEN CRAIGAN: John Lambie had a few whiskies one night with Partick Thistle in Blackpool because he says it helps him sleep, but he left his key in the door. Gerry 'Mullet' Britton spotted it. He went in with a couple of the boys and tried to take the bed – with John in it – down to the dining room but couldn't get it through the door. So instead, they got a big wardrobe and stuck it outside his door so that when John opened it he couldn't get out. When he got up in the morning he walked straight into it – there must have been about half a dozen of us behind the wardrobe laughing. But he got his own back at training when he absolutely bleached us by running us solid for two hours on the beach – it was worth it though.

LEE MAKEL: David Batty and Mike Newell used to room together and they were always causing havoc. We were staying in one hotel and they cut out the spy hole to my door and stuck the hose of a fire extinguisher through it. They soaked my room while I was in it. I had no idea what was going on.

MARK MCGEOWN (Stirling Albion, Airdrie, Ayr): Somebody phoned up Andy Paterson at Stirling and pretended to be a journalist telling him he had been voted player of the month. He was told to go to Ibrox to collect his award. I don't know how far he got but I think he was definitely on his way to the ground to get it before he realised something was up.

STEVIE FERGUSON: Ian Maxwell once sent a letter to George Shaw, telling him he was nominated as Player of the Year while he was at Ross County. George actually scored something like seventeen goals that season and it wouldn't have been a surprise if he really was on the list. After George had organised the number of tickets he wanted, he phoned the PFA and found out it was a wind-up. It was a touchy subject back then and in training he put in a few heavy tackles.

BARRY ROBSON: I remember when Paul Gascoigne stuck two fish in Gordon Durie's club car. He hid one under the passenger seat and when Gordon found it he thought that was the joke over. But of course Gazza had hidden another one in the car and Gordon, for the life of him, couldn't understand why the smell was still there. It is the best wind-up ever. At Caley, Duncan Shearer once unscrewed the licence plates on Scott McLean's new car and put them on upside down during training.

STEVEN THOMPSON (Dundee United, Rangers): We were staying in a hotel and I took a room on the ground floor. I made the mistake of leaving my window open when I went out and David Bowman totally trashed the place. He tore the curtains off the wall and threw the bed covers everywhere. Then he filled a bath up and chucked in all my clothes. He filled my toothpaste tube with shower gel. I was devastated when I saw the mess – but what really hurt was discovering he'd stolen the tube of wine gums I had stashed away. I myself try not to play too many pranks, although I used to spray messages with shaving foam on Maurice Malpas' car until he went mad at me.

CHRIS MCGROARTY: Gerry Britton pulled a cracker of a wind-up on Ivo den Bieman. Big Ivo used to have this silly-looking Citroen 2CV. It was clapped out, had a roof that leaked and looked silly, but it was still his pride and joy. Gerry nicked his keys one day and drove it right on to the pitch. Ivo was in the dressing room and knew nothing about it until he went to go home. He thought someone had stolen his car – as if.

MIKE TEASDALE: Paul Cherry was always playing practical jokes. He once went to a dentist and got a set of false teeth made so he could come into training with them in. He was always buying silly clothes from Oxfam and places like that and turns up to games with them on.

GLYNN HURST: Darren Sheridan was the ultimate wind-up merchant. He got me big style the night before I made my debut at Southend. We were staying at a hotel and he managed to get a key for my room. He then got a bucket of water and ice and stuck it above my door. When I opened the door I was soaking. And when I went to bed I found he'd left a little trail of melted ice cubes there. My bed was soaking and all the lads thought I'd had an accident in it.

BILLY MCNEILL: We had these travelling blazers with massive pockets and time and again on planes I'd stick my hand in my pocket on the way off to discover Bobby Lennox and Jimmy Johnstone had filled it with mustard and tomato sauce. They were a couple of pains in the a**e. I also hated it down at Seamill when we were playing golf. They would hide over the hill at holes and throw your ball into the gorse bushes. You'd come over and they'd pretend they'd just been out for a walk. They spent hours hurling balls all over the course.

BARRY FERGUSON (Rangers, Scotland): We were with Blackburn pre-season and played a belter of a prank on the masseur Kevin who just loves his sleep. Every one of us bought an alarm clock then we broke into his room and planked them everywhere from his toilet cabinet to his air-conditioning duct. They were primed to go off every hour and he was going mental all through the night. He was running down the corridor next morning shouting "B*****ds!" Classic.

ROBERT SNODGRASS: I rang Michael Gardyne up pretending to be a Glasgow hardman who was after him because he'd been seeing my wife behind my back. He was absolutely bricking it. I think he tried to get his own back because I had a lot of private numbers come up on my phone.

DEREK MCINNES: We were on a trip to Canada with Rangers when one day, half the boys went to see the sights, like Niagara Falls, while the rest of us went drinking. Craig Moore was one of the lads who wanted to take holiday snaps and when he joined us later we wound him up by telling him that Jon Bon Jovi came into the bar we'd been in and gave an impromptu performance, singing all his hits. Oz is a huge fan and was gutted, especially when we said Bon Jovi invited Coisty up on stage to sing a duet. Weeks later Oz came up to me in training and said he was still gutted he'd missed it. To this day he believes it happened.

RICKY GILLIES: Every day at St Mirren, I would soak all the players with the cold hose after training. When the lads go in the showers I chase after them with it. It sounds terrible, but it's a good laugh seeing lots of grown men hiding in one cubicle completely naked. Another impressive wind-up was when we were down in Blackpool. All the lads went off the bus to get something to eat and Scott McKenzie left his mobile behind. I started playing about with it and decided to send a text message to Alex Totten, his former manager at Falkirk. I typed in the words "I love you . . . please take me back to Brockville".

KEVIN GALLACHER: I never saw it but was told about it on my Scotland travels. It happened to a Celtic player – who can't be named – who had just joined the club. He was polishing boots when the older players told him he had to use elbow grease. They told him the supermarket sold it. The player was looking for it on the shelves and the other players turned up to laugh at him.

TONY BULLOCK (Dundee United, Dundee, Ross County): We travelled to Edinburgh to meet up for a game but some of us had to stop for the toilet. There were no toilets about so we peed in a car park. When we got back to Dundee, Grant Brebner and Stevie Crawford told Barry Robson that the police had called and he was the only one spotted on CCTV doing the toilet. Barry believed them and was all concerned about what to do and what fine he'd have to pay. It got to the stage where he was ready to jump in the car to Edinburgh to hand himself in until Grant and Stevie confessed.

JOHNNY WHELAN (Queen's Park): Some of the Queen's Park boys got hold of firecrackers and smoke bombs and put them under my car. When I came out of training, I thought something was wrong and started emptying stuff out of my car. I realised the engine wasn't running then noticed Steve Canning, Ross Clarke and Tony Quinn standing there laughing.

KEVIN TINDAL: I remember a spat between Andy Gibson and Craig Yeats at Peterhead. Andy did something to Craig and as revenge he got some construction foam and stuck it in his shoes.

The foam solidified and there is nothing you can do to get rid of it – you can't pick it or dissolve it so the shoes were ruined.

KENNY ARTHUR: Gerry Britton got Adam Strachan a cracker. Adam had only just arrived at Partick and Gerry told him to go out and check the undersoil heating was working by feeling the grass. Adam went out feeling the centre circle, the penalty spot and everywhere else to see if the heat was on. I think he twigged when one of the boys fell over from laughing.

DANNY CUNNING: We pulled a prank on a journalist at the *Edinburgh Evening News*. He came to our training ground one day while the rest of the team were having a meeting with the manager. We told him there was a press conference with Tommy Burns, who was being linked with the club. He burst into the room in the middle of this meeting and was promptly kicked out by Davie Hay.

GRAHAM BAYNE: Liam Fox used to come into training early and take your car keys and hide your car. I remember John McCormack would pull tricks on the young skillseekers at Dundee by sending them round the shops to get tartan paint and light-bulbs for the stadium floodlights.

CHRISTIAN KALVENES (Dundee United): Norwegian TV played a great prank on Charlie Miller. They set it up so that he was interviewed by police about his car being used in a robbery and was asked if he knew anything about it. Then all of a sudden the police had this guy in handcuffs who was said to have been involved – and he shouted out: "Charlie, don't tell them anything!" Charlie was totally bemused – but then the guy escaped into a car and drove off leaving Charlie on his own and having to answer some questions. Then from out of nowhere, a camera crew appeared – Charlie took it very well.

MIKE FRASER: My mate Mark Holmes phoned me up recently pretending to be some agent of a company wanting me to do a commercial for a local pottery company because I was a local celebrity. He wanted me to walk into the shop with my gloves on and when someone knocked over something I was supposed to dive and catch it. I was pretty excited because I thought I was going to get paid good money for it and I even told the boys. But then Mark turned up with a video camera and he filmed my disappointment when he told me it was him.

TOM PARRATT: Richard Offiong borrowed my phone and started texting Neil Taggart pretending to be a girl he had met on a night out. Neil didn't have my number, so it worked a treat. We kept up the pretence for about three or four days. The plan was to arrange to meet Neil and we would get all the boys to turn up – but then we were rumbled.

PAUL SHEERIN (Ayr, Caley Thistle, Aberdeen, St Johnstone): At St Johnstone, we would play for cakes at training on a Friday. I have a sweet tooth and love my fudge and cream doughnuts. But someone stole my cake and I got a picture message of it on someone's dashboard with a ransom text demanding £1 million. It was from Jamie McCluskey and Gary Irvine. I then put my cake in different hiding places after that.

DEAN HOLDEN: A mate sent me a text saying to bet on his pal's horse called Norfolk En Chance. He said the odds were 14–1 and that he was in the know. I told everyone in the dressing room and my friends about it. Eventually I got a text full of swear words from one person saying it was a wind-up. I didn't realise what it said when you read the name fast. I'm sure some of the Irish boys at Falkirk tried to put money on it.

TAM SCOBBIE: Keeper John Hutchison cut the toes out of Eddie May's socks. Eddie didn't notice and stuck his foot right through. He went mental and chased JC who tried to lock himself in the boot room and was shouting he was so sorry.

TRENT MCCLENAHAN: When I was at MK Dons one of the coaching staff got a fish and put it underneath one of the players' car seat. No amount of air fresheners could make his car smell any better. It was notorious there and you had to watch out for everything. Your socks would get cut, Deep Heat put in your boxers and this coach even put grass cuttings in someone's air conditioning vent in a car. He was switched on.

DUNCAN SHEARER: It was my first involvement with the Scotland squad and we were staying at a hotel near Greenock. Maurice Malpas told me there was a meeting just before dinner down by the river because it was such a nice night. I turned up and of course there was no one there and the meeting was actually at the hotel, so I was well stitched up. I walked in sheepishly as Andy Roxburgh was chatting to the players.

MURRAY DAVIDSON (Livingston, St Johnstone): Robert Snodgrass and Graham Dorrans were supposed to pay fine money, but they didn't cough up. We waited months for it. Colin Stewart was in charge of the fine money, so to get them to pay he jacked their cars up and stole a wheel from each of them until they paid up. Then they got their wheels back.

GARY ARBUCKLE: Sean McKenna thought it would be good to get involved in a wet boxers contest in a night out with the Clyde boys in Glasgow. He had water chucked over him and danced about. Next day, Joe Miller got wind of it and drafted a letter as if it was from Strathclyde Police saying they wanted to question him about an incident of indecent exposure.

GILLIAN DONALDSON (Morton Chief Executive): Morton were due to play Elgin and we had travelled up the night before to stay in a hotel. It was Valentine's Day and when I came down the players had set up a table for two in the dining room, with Valentine's cards, flowers and presents, for the manager John McCormack and myself. Everyone else in the hotel thought it was serious, but John and I just sat and ate our dinner.

CRAIG BROWN: Scotland were preparing for the 1986 World Cup in Mexico. I was next door to Alex Ferguson in a hotel in New Mexico. I heard him ranting and raving after we'd come in from a few pints. He chapped on my door and asked if my lights were working. He said he couldn't get his on. It turned out the boys – one of whom, I suspect, was Charlie Nicholas – had unscrewed them and put cling film over the toilet. Alex, of course, had gone to the toilet and been caught out.

10

Hungover in a Foreign Land

MAGALUF is the footballer's favourite haunt at the end of the season. The boozy bender abroad is a bonding session to celebrate the end of the season, but beer and footballers sometimes don't mix, as the following proves . . .

BARRY ROBSON: I went to Prague for my best mate Jamie's stag do. We had him drinking Absinthe, which is the strongest alcohol around. We filled him and when he went in to use a Portaloo we kicked it over. He was jammed in but when we eventually managed to get him out he was covered in s*** and blue detergent.

GERRY FARRELL: Kenny Black turned up for an Airdrie holiday in Magaluf with his clothes in a Tesco bag. He had just been released by the club and spent the holiday man-marking Alex Totten trying to get a deal at Falkirk. The boozers would close at 3am and he'd be holding Totty's hand when the lights went on.

KENNY CLARK (Referee): I was in Morocco with Les Mottram for a World Cup qualifier and after the game we ended up at a bar mitzvah in the hotel. Les got taken up to dance with a belly dancer. She danced all round Les while he shuffled uncomfortably beside her.

TREVOR MOLLOY: I was part of the Dublin District Under-19 team which won a holiday to Portugal to watch Ireland play there. We were in a pub one night and I somehow ended up on the stage with a transvestite who was looking for a volunteer. The ladyboy then had a real snake and put it in my mouth! My team-mates must have egged me on although I did have a couple of drinks too.

STEPHEN SWIFT: When we were over in Marbella with Stranraer, the keeper Kenny Meechan accidentally peed on Michael Moore's leg, so Michael decided to get him back. As Kenny was lying back relaxing in the Jacuzzi, Michael peed on his forehead while we all watched. It was absolutely hilarious.

DAVID GRAHAM (Stranraer, Hamilton, Dunfermline): In Marbella with Stranraer, we'd had a few bevvies and six of us went back to our rooms. Lee Sharp and Frazer Wright had got up to play golf early doors and the balcony window was shut and Sharpy had shut the room door. That left me, Stephen Swift, Kevin Finlayson and Derek Wingate. But when we woke up, somehow Stephen Marshall was standing in front of us with nothing on but a leather jacket and a pair of shades. He was walking back and forth like a robot at the bottom of the bed saying: "I will get you

Sarah Connors," from *The Terminator*. How he got into the room none of us know to this day.

STEPHEN DOCHERTY (Airdrie): The Airdrie boys were in Magaluf when David Dunn made the fatal mistake of falling asleep by the pool. We stuck ten cigarettes in his mouth and lit them so every time he breathed in the fags would flare up and when he breathed out there was lots of smoke. We just left him there. He ended up with a sore throat.

GERRY COLLINS: We were in Benidorm with the Partick players and we were drinking in the pub. John Lambie was absolutely legless so I told him to go back to the hotel. The next morning John was in his bed with his trousers all filthy, shoes dirty, his brand new Pringle jumper torn and his face all scratched. He said he'd been mugged and had £1,000 spending cash stolen from him. The chairman Jim Oliver gave him some more money for the rest of the holiday. On the last day, John found a sock with a grand in it and admitted it was his money. He told us he'd actually fallen into some bushes. He'd been too embarrassed to tell us so that's why he'd made up the story about being mugged.

STEVE PATERSON: In 1982, I played a season in Hong Kong and one day we took a hovercraft to a Portuguese colony called Macau which is the Las Vegas of the Far East. We went to the casino and not only did I lose my money but I lost my mates and missed my hovercraft back. I ended up marooned on the island for three days with no money during the monsoon season. I was up to my knees in mud and no one could speak English. I used to sleep at night on the couches in the casinos but a Chinese policeman would whack me with a stick. I eventually found a dollar coin in a slot machine so I phoned my Scottish mate Paul Rodgers and he came across and rescued me.

JOHN HUGHES: Simon Stainrod was once decked by a night-club bouncer in Magaluf when he wouldn't return someone's hat. The closest I came was when I had a go at Frank Connor at training but he turned round, gave me that look and said: "You think this stick is for helping me walk? It would look quite funny sticking out your a**e." I just stuck my head down and shut up. That's the only time I have been left speechless. The next day I apologised.

CHRIS HILLCOAT: One night in Tenerife, I tried to keep up with Crawford Baptie in the drinking stakes, which turned out to be the silliest thing I've ever done. When I got home, I went in the lift and it got stuck. Paul McKenzie and Gary Clark heard me screaming but they just laughed. They managed to get the lift doors open slightly. All they could see was me trying to use the phone and burst out laughing. They eventually dragged me out and Paul Chalmers pulled me along by the ankles. I ended up with carpet burns on my chin.

STEPHEN CRAIGAN: When Partick won the Second Division title, we went to Ayia Napa for a week and we drank the whole time. Most of the guys hired mopeds and tried to drive them after drinking. When we went to the Car Wash nightclub Scott

McLean and Allan Moore turned up with their jeans and shirts ripped because they had both crashed their bikes. Another day I went to kick a ball at the side of the pool but slipped and smashed my elbow.

JIM DUFFY: I was with a few football mates who went to Tenerife for a holiday. For a laugh, we decided to tell everyone around the pool area that we'd been named Best Binmen in Britain and had got the trip as first prize. We said we were nominated by the people in our street because we were really quiet and never woke anyone up. On another end-of-season trip with Dundee, I accidentally poisoned Noel Blake when I made him down a shot of washing detergent in a drinking game. He was sick everywhere because there was ammonia in whatever it was I'd given him – I blamed Cowboy McCormack.

TOM STEVEN: I was once so drunk at a Player of the Year awards in Australia, I couldn't go up and collect the trophy I'd won. Because it was on live TV they gave it to the second-placed player and I ended up getting thrown out.

CRAIG FARNAN: We were on Stuart Garden's stag do in Dublin when he was set to marry Jocky Scott's daughter. One minute we were in the pub drinking and the next thing I saw Stuart standing there naked apart from his shoes. He knew that we were going to strip him but ended up doing it himself to save us the trouble.

SCOTT THOMSON (Raith, Dunfermline): I had been drinking so much on holiday in Magaluf, I started to hallucinate! I swear I saw someone's feet next to me moving when there was no one in the room. I told the others guys but they just looked at me as if I was crazy.

PETER HETHERSTON: When you go to Magaluf on a bender it takes you a week to recover. Even boys who don't drink get carried away. The funny thing is seeing all the wives at the airport shaking their heads when they see the state of their men. I've had many daggers from my wife Roslyn. Steven Cody chatted to a girl who was reading her book – she had almost finished it when Steven tore out the last five pages and threw it in the water.

GED BRANNAN (Motherwell): We used to go to Magaluf every year with Tranmere and I remember one time Shaun Garnett went missing for three hours. We eventually saw him walking up the street dressed as a WOMAN with a blonde wig and make-up! He did it for a laugh but liked the new look so much he kept it for the rest of the day. Shaun is a 6ft 3in monster so you can imagine what he looked like.

KEVIN DRINKELL: I was in Zimbabwe when we went on a tour with Coventry. I was drinking one night and ended up in a tin hut beside a mansion with some guys I met. But I could easily have disappeared and no one would have known what happened to me.

DAVIE NICHOLLS: We had an end of season trip in Magaluf the year we won promotion from Division Two at Clydebank. As you can imagine we were on a high and were making plenty of noise. The hotel manager came up to complain and asked who the gaffer was. Just at that moment, the lift door opened to show Gordon Chisholm pushing Ian McCall in a wheelchair because he'd had a wee bit too much. We all laughed and pointed to say, "He is." The hotel guy shook his head in despair.

NIGEL PEPPER (Aberdeen): I was on holiday in the Dominican Republic with my dad, brother-in-law and friend and we were playing cricket on the beach. My mate decided to go and get the beers and he walked back casually carrying four pints of lager. He kept coming towards us and the ball flew in his direction. He couldn't resist trying to catch it and started running towards it. Then he went flying and spilled all the beer.

NIGEL QUASHIE (Scotland): There was a player called Matthew Brazier at QPR and when we were on pre-season in Italy, he got absolutely blitzed one night. He fell asleep and they shaved one of his eyebrows off. Matthew was rough as hell and slogging through the running so hard that it took him TWO DAYS to look in a mirror again and realise what had happened. We were all p***ing ourselves, it was quality.

DAVID GRAHAM: During a boozy night in Benidorm with Stranraer, Frazer Wright and I got hold of some workies' jackets. We went out and took turns in directing traffic on the main road.

DEAN KEENAN (Morton, Ayr): After missing out on promotion with Morton, we went on a four-day bender then woke up thinking it was really hot. Alex Williams and I then suddenly remembered we had gone to Ibiza.

JIMMY CALDERWOOD (Dunfermline, Aberdeen): We were in Australia with Birmingham and a few of us went on the lash. Kenny Burns and I were walking through Surfers' Paradise at 3am when we saw one of those beach-side trampoline things and sneaked in. There were six in a row and we tried to do them all, lost our balance and scratched all our faces. The police turned up and the manager was not happy.

STEVIE MURRAY: I'm told when Killie were in Dublin I challenged Stevie Fulton to a drinking contest and let's just say I ended up lying down in a cobbled street in the city centre needing a nappy. I remember some of the lads putting Euro coins in my drink and me swallowing them. I was on everything that night, including brandy.

DEREK MCINNES: After winning both eight and nine in a row with Rangers, the club sent the Scottish contingent to Toronto on an all-expenses trip. It was sponsored by Labatts beer so we were never short of alcohol. One day we were so drunk, Coisty, Charlie Miller and I all did a bungee jump together – the three of us on one cord!

STEVIE HISLOP (Caley Thistle, Ross County, Raith): I was in Ayia Napa in a pub called Bedrocks with my mates from Edinburgh and tried to steal a novelty *Flintstones* bike. A bouncer – dressed up as Fred – then threw me off the bike and punched me in the face. I ended up with a cut lip.

MARK CRILLY: There was a group of us in Ibiza and it was just birds and booze. But the place is full of gay men and transvestites. I remember Keith Lasley being chatted up by another bloke and running away.

COLIN NISH (Dunfermline, Kilmarnock, Hibs): We went on a Magaluf trip with the boys. I don't think we ate anything – it was just drink. We would wake up and still be drunk from the night before and go straight out drinking. I remember sitting by the pool when David Lilley said he was going to the toilet but he ended up diving head first into the shallow end of the pool and split his head open.

FRAZER WRIGHT (Kilmarnock stopper): Neil Watt took the whole Stranraer team to Benidorm and it was just sheer mayhem for five days. Kevin Finlayson actually ended up getting a few stitches after Kevin Gaughan did a clothesline wresting move on him – that's when you stick your arm out and someone runs into it. Kevin had it done to him but he cracked his head off a window and went to hospital.

STEVIE MILNE: I was in Ayia Napa with a dozen of the Dundee boys. One morning after a big drinking session, I got a moped and flew up and down the streets doing wheelies. Derek Soutar did the same, but he crashed his into a bin lorry.

COLIN STEWART: I can only remember bits and pieces of my stag do in Magaluf for five days with some of the boys and we had a night out kitted out in full keeper's gear. We were going down the main strip doing warm-up exercises, then I got jumped and the boys stripped me to just my gloves. They tried to claim I stripped myself but I want to put that straight.

ALAN GOW: I shared a room with Mark Roberts in Magaluf when he picked up an infection and ended up looking like Shrek. He looked terrible and wouldn't leave the hotel for the whole holiday. He was paranoid even at the airport when we were going home, covering up his face.

DAVID PROCTOR: The Caley Thistle boys were on a trip to Magaluf when Roy McBain went AWOL. No one could find him. It turned out he was worse for wear and went to the hotel next door, got his key for a room with the same number and slept on the bed. He got a fright when an elderly couple found him in their room. They called the police and he was escorted out.

DAVID ELEBERT: I once saw a bar brawl in Knoxville. We were in the place enjoying a quiet drink when it kicked off out of nowhere. I'm telling you, it was like a scene from an old western movie. One person hit another guy and it just erupted with everyone joining in. There were tables and chairs flying everywhere.

STEPHEN SWIFT: After we won the Third Division with Stranraer, Neil Watt took us to Spain as a reward. We were near Marbella and it was just four days of madness. I remember on the way back I was so bad I was in the toilet on the plane throwing up. The stewardess kept banging the door telling me to get back to my seat for take-off but I couldn't. I remember Dundee United were on the same plane. If Ian McCall knew it was me being sick he probably wouldn't have signed me for Queen of the South.

CRAIG SAMSON: I was in Magaluf with a few pals, including Andy Dowie, at the time when France beat England with two late goals. Andy decided to get French t-shirts and we were given abuse and threatened with beatings about fifteen times. We had been drinking for five days straight and then another five days after that.

JIM LAUCHLAN: We went away to Malaga with Kilmarnock during the winter shutdown. Bobby Williamson said we could have a few beers after training, but told us to make sure we were up for 8am to train otherwise we'd be fined. Everyone turned up except for Bobby, Gerry McCabe and Jim Clark who'd all slept in.

COLIN CAMERON (Raith, Hearts, Wolves, Scotland): Just after we won the Coca Cola Cup with Raith Rovers in 1994, we went to Magaluf and Jimmy Nicholl said we had to train to justify us being there. But that was just a cover and we were fined if we didn't go out at night and fined if we returned to the hotel before 3am. But we were training at around 10am every morning and if you were sick during training you were fined. All the money went into the kitty for the next night.

Laugh Out Loud

MORE comical moments from the world of the footballer — they really are just big kids!

GORDON MCQUEEN (Scotland): Lou Macari liked a laugh and one time we played a joke on our assistant manager Mick Brown when we were in Montego Bay. He liked a smoke so would always have his verandah doors open. We decided to catch a peacock and stick it in his room so it was there when he woke up.

GERRY COLLINS: I dropped off Hamilton's legendary foul-mouthed fan Fergie round the corner from Parkhead when I was on my way to see Tommy Burns. I was waiting in my car, and out of the corner of my eye saw Fergie walk up to the front entrance as Mo Johnston walked out. Fergie kneeled, blessed himself and shouted: "Gerry, look at these Fenian b******s."

JIMMY NICHOLL: Davie Cooper had just been recalled to the Scotland squad and Ally was to pick him up in Motherwell at six for a team meeting in Glasgow half an hour later. Coops waited until twenty past before deciding to call a taxi. Just then Coisty's car screeches up. Coops gives Ally an earful saying: "It's okay for you, Andy Roxburgh likes you, but I need to impress." Ally replies: "Calm down big man, that's the earliest I've ever been late for anyone!"

TAM MACDONALD: Willie Thompson cracked me up. We were getting ready for a Scottish Cup quarter-final and you could cut the tension with a knife. Willie stripped off his suit and had on a leather basque, suspenders and stockings underneath! Classic, and we went on to win.

CHRIS STRAIN: Craig Conway was having a fancy dress party for his twenty-first and brought in a dress his girlfriend was going to wear. It was a sexy maid's outfit or something. There was a board meeting on so I put the dress on and took a tray of sandwiches to the boardroom. The chief executive nearly had a fit and ushered me away in disbelief. I think he took a sandwich, though.

MARK REILLY (Kilmarnock, St Mirren): Ally McCoist played a great trick on Jim Lauchlan after Jim bought a new convertible which Bobby Williamson wasn't impressed with. Ally knew this and when he, Jim and I travelled to training, Ally said it would be a good idea if we turned up with the top down, blaring loud music, and drove on the grass towards the players and spun around. Ally told him everyone would love that so he did it. The players scattered and Bobby was absolutely raging. Ally simply said: "I told him he shouldn't have done it boss."

RYAN MCGUFFIE: Ronnie McQuilter was at Gretna when Rowan Alexander put his name on the bench as he wrote the team up on the board. Ronnie, in his strong Glasgow accent, said: "Just scrub that name aff a there and if you don't I'll no play again ya ****. You couldnae manage a Subbuteo team." Rowan didn't utter a word, but wiped Ronnie's name off and stuck his own down. Ronnie just walked off.

ALEX KEDDIE: Michael Gardyne was wrapped up in cling film by Kevin McKinlay and Craig Samson. He was made to bounce out of the club and ended up falling and getting a carpet burn on the side of his face.

BARRY MCLAUGHLIN: The day after Frank McAvennie came back to St Mirren, we arranged to meet in a pub. Forty minutes passed and there was no sign of Macca, then out of the corner of my eye I saw him nestled between two darlings smoking a cigar – typical Macca.

CHRIS KILLEN: Les Chapman was the old Manchester City kitman. One day he put on a black and yellow rugby top and a black shower cap, pretended he was a bumblebee and ran through the training session humming and buzzing. He also once dressed up as Hitler and waved goodbye to us as we left on the team bus for an away game. He forgot Eyal Berkovic was on board. Eyal was fuming.

GERRY COLLINS: Wee Colin McGlashan took a knock to the head in a game for Partick. John Lambie shouted over to the physio John Hart to see what was wrong and Harty replied: "He doesn't know who he is – he's concussed." Quick as a flash John responded: "Well tell him he's Pele and get him back on." The whole place fell about laughing.

JOHN HUGHES: Mo Johnston had just signed for Falkirk and I was driving him and John Clark home. Big John threw Mo's new club blazer and flannels out the window for a laugh. We didn't stop the car either. Another funny moment was watching Brian Rice suffer in the heat of Magaluf. He spent the whole week under an umbrella – we call him the white polar bear.

BRIAN MCGINTY: The funniest chat-up attempt I saw was a pal of a pal going up to a girl at a golf club and introducing himself as "Bond, James Bond". The girl just replied: "Off, **** off!"

DEAN KEENAN: Iain Russell, Scott McLaughlin, Kieran McAnespie and I were travel partners. We were stopped at a red light when our favourite song came on. It's that 'American Boy' one by Estelle, so we all got out and started dancing. The traffic stopped to watch, everyone was tooting their horns and shouting. It was amazing.

STUART TAYLOR: During a Falkirk reserve match at Brockville, the ball was heading out towards the dugout when Brian Rice came out to get it. But he didn't see a bucket lying there and got his foot stuck in it. He went as red as his hair but luckily for him only a few people saw it.

LEE MAIR: Watching Jamie Langfield get a tattoo was probably the funniest thing I've seen because he started crying and then fainted! I was in stitches. When he woke up he was white as a sheet. It put me off getting a tattoo.

DANNY CUNNING: We were playing Sturm Graz at Almondvale in our first venture into Europe. You have a meeting with a UEFA official to discuss various things and one of the problems was that our shorts clashed with the Austrians. They didn't have spare ones so we were told we had to wear our purple shorts with gold jerseys. When Jim Leishman heard he went mental and burst into the room shouting: "No way are we wearing purple with gold!" Then he stormed out. The UEFA delegate just said: "Don't worry, I've dealt with grumpy kit-men before."

JIMMY NICHOLL: Manchester United were in Yugoslavia preparing for a big European match with Red Star Belgrade when the two Dubliners Paddy Roche and Gerry Daly fell foul of Lou Macari. He nicked their keys – for a door that can only be unlocked from the outside – and their phone to stop any cries of help to the porter. The whole squad congregated outside their room and heard Paddy shout: "Where's the bloody key Gerry?" who replied: "You had it!" Then they decided to phone for help, but of course when they couldn't find the phone, they were done by Lou. We kept them in there while we went for a walk and returned to find Paddy had smoked all his cigars and left Toblerone packets on the floor.

OWEN COYLE: Stewart Kennedy – who lost five goals to England at Wembley –was in goals at Dumbarton when a fan behind the goal shouted: "Kennedy, you're nothing but a big dumpling. I saw the five goals you lost to England." Quick as a flash he replied: "You lucky b*****d – I never saw any of them!"

JOHN MCCORMACK: I used to have a great laugh playing with Frank McDougall. I remember one time we went on a trip to Finland with St Mirren and he was conked out after having a few beers. One lad decided it would be a laugh to tie his big toes together with string. He tied them really tightly and we just sat there watching a half-asleep Frank wondering why he couldn't wriggle his feet apart.

IAN DURRANT (Rangers, Kilmarnock): I was at a Rolling Stones concert at Wembley one night and wangled my way backstage to be two feet from Jerry Hall. After a few Buds I was ready with the legendary Durrant patter but when she turned round to speak I had a chicken wing in my mouth. I don't think she was too impressed.

STEVEN MCGARRY (St Mirren, Ross County, Motherwell): I roomed with Barry Lavety when we were up in Inverness. Late at night, we went for a walk in the hotel. We found a fire extinguisher and Basher decided to let it off, thinking liquid would skoosh out from it. I pushed open a room door and he fed the nozzle through it before turning it on – only for a white POWDER to come out. The room belonged to Junior Mendes and Ludo Roy and when we switched the light on they were completely white. We were all laughing so much that we woke people up and the hotel manager got a bit annoyed. In the end, the club had to pay for the damage, although they never actually found out who the guilty man was.

ANDY THOMSON (Queen of the South, Partick, Falkirk): I was watching a reserve game and a big Nigerian lad called Dominic Iorfa had been hit in the face with the ball and asked for some water. Somebody threw a water bottle on the pitch and he squirted it in his eye and face but then spent the next ten minutes screaming because it was in fact orange squash in the bottle. I was in stitches.

PETER CANERO (Kilmarnock): I was sharing a room with my Kilmarnock team-mate Shaun Dillon while we were with the Scotland Under-21s and we had a flight the next morning at 8am. I got his mobile and changed the time on it and woke him up at 2am to tell him to get up as we had to leave. He ended up going for a shower while I went back to bed killing myself laughing.

RODDY MCKENZIE (Hearts, Livingston): Robbie Neilson was driving a group of us to training at Hearts once when he spotted a guy in a smart suit walking past a huge puddle in the road. He timed it to perfection and gave this poor guy a complete soaking.

STEVIE HISLOP: A common practical joke at County was someone would stick a condom on someone else's shoulder on a night out.

ROBERT CONNOR: Our old physio at Ayr United was Willie Wallace. He was a great guy and would sometimes take the training. He was leading us on a run around Somerset Park when we all jumped behind a wall and hid from him. He kept running for half the pitch before he realised we weren't there.

CRAIG NELSON: Marvyn Wilson's lasso dance is legendary. It is difficult to describe but it's the most hilarious thing I've ever seen. We had a Christmas night out at Ayr and from across the room Marvyn started his dance. He pretends to lasso someone and pulls himself along to you while shuffling his feet. Another funny thing has been watching Chris Hay trying to header a ball.

RICHIE FORAN: Roddy Collins once gave the wrong player at Carlisle a contract for three years. He confused him with another player who had the same first name. He realised his mistake and had to tell him.

TONY BULLOCK: Dundee United were 3–0 down at Hearts when Billy Dodds tried something fancy. He started playing keepie-up then went to volley the ball over his head but it ended up smashing him in the face and knocked him out. We were all dying to laugh but we couldn't because of the scoreline at the time.

ALEX WILLIAMS: In my West Park days, we went to Holland. Some of us were on a boat and coming towards a bridge. As Willie Stewart grabbed the bridge, Joe Boyle and I pushed the boat back and left him hanging there. We went back but instead of rescuing him we pulled his shorts down.

KENNY CLARK: Hugh Dallas did a great impression of Eddie the Eagle at Dunblane Hydro. A few of the officials went looking for a pub after a meeting when Hugh suggested we cut across the grass but myself and Colin Hardie told him not to be stupid as it was raining. Hugh took two steps and then just disappeared into the darkness with a scream before re-emerging covered in mud.

SCOTT HIGGINS: When I was with Queensland Roar, a ball came over the top of Reece Tollenare as he chased it. He kept his eye on it but didn't see the spare set of goalposts off the pitch and ran straight into them. It was funny at first but then we realised he'd knocked himself out! It was quite serious and he had concussion.

STEVIE MILNE: Graham Bayne was playing for the Dundee Under-21s and had just scored a hat-trick. He was being subbed and started walking off applauding the claps he was getting. But he then tripped on a metal hook on the ground and fell flat on his face.

COLIN STEWART: I was in Magaluf one summer when my wife's cousin's husband Craig 'TK Maxx' MacDonald got up to go to the toilet. I watched him walk straight into a mirror and then apologise to himself. I also find it funny that my brother-in-law Chris Strain was booked for Ayr before coming off the subs' bench.

TREVOR MOLLOY: When Motherwell played Celtic, Richie Foran said that Shunsuke Nakamura had nut-megged him in their previous game and he said it wasn't going to happen again. Within ten minutes of the game, Nakamura had nut-megged him twice. I was sitting in the stand with Danny Murphy and Paul Keegan and we were laughing our heads off.

GARY DEMPSEY: Noel Hunt and Richie Byrne were in the showers at Dunfermline and I soaked them with a bucket of cold water. Then the three of us started throwing water around for ten minutes. Noel was chasing Richie with a big bin of cold water and waited behind the door. When the door opened, Noel threw the water over Billy Kirkwood who had just walked in. He wasn't amused.

FRANK MCGARVEY: Vic Davidson caused a funny scene when we were playing in Seattle – he asked the referee what happened if the ball hit the ceiling of the dome. The referee didn't know and looked up but the ceiling was miles high.

JOHN BURRIDGE: I smacked Alex Miller before a game against Airdrie. In my second season there, we were playing at Broomfield but it was a wet night and I wanted to wear my own plastic jacket. Alex told me I had to wear the club jersey, so five minutes before kick-off I smacked him in the mouth and he was on the floor. Next thing, my legs went after Murdo MacLeod hit me on the head with a mobile phone. Alex got up and tried to ring the SFA, but he didn't realise the phone was broken. We ended up laughing about it.

JIM BETT: When Scotland played France in a match in Marseille in 1985, Neil Simpson came off the bench near the end but instead of taking up his position, he ran straight to Michel Platini and asked him if he could get his jersey after the game. And he did.

PAT STANTON: Celtic were playing Red Star Belgrade in Australia and I got sent off for punching one of their forwards near the end of the game. Jock asked why a player of my experience couldn't wait ten or fifteen minutes before I got him back. I told him there were only two minutes to go and Jock just said: "You're quite right then!"

GARY STEVENS (Rangers, England): When I first signed for Rangers I had no idea about the rivalry with Celtic. I had a snooker table put into my house in Bridge of Weir and the company who installed it were of a Rangers persuasion. They actually didn't want to give me green baize or a green ball.

STEWART HILLIS (Professor and Scotland doctor): At the time when we weren't getting results under Berti Vogts, our goalie coach Jim Stewart said: "The Panzers are coming over the horizon," which I don't think was the best thing to say in the presence of Berti.

SCOTT CHAPLAIN: I was on a YTS at Ayr United and it was the last day of the season before the summer holidays. We were told to paint the boot room but two of the lads, Aidan McVeigh and Mark Ferry, waited at the side of the door and when Chris Foley walked in, they painted the side of his head and hair. Campbell Money came in and went absolutely mental. He brought us in for some hard running the next day.

EAMONN BANNON: I was with the Scotland squad in Canada and there was a great prank Roy Aitken would do where he got a $20 bill and would stick see-through tape onto it and leave it on the ground at the airport. Then we would stand back and watch people try to pick it up and Roy would yank it away from them. We did that everywhere we went.

ROBBIE RAESIDE: At Raith, kids like Jason Dair and Stevie Crawford would hide in the laundry baskets. When the senior players like Gordon Dalziel and Peter Hetherston walked by and reached inside they would be hauled in. Peter is a hard man but he s**t himself.

MARC TWADDLE: Falkirk were playing Hearts and Liam Craig had a spat with Paul Hartley. Liam ended up having a go at the ref and Paul asked him: "What do you get paid for? Moaning?"

Liam just replied: "What do you get paid for?" Moments later, Paul scored, ran back, winked at Liam and said: "That's what I get paid for, wee man!"

DON HUTCHISON: I used to work as a forklift driver before I went full-time. There was a boy in on work experience and the manager sent him to B&Q and asked him to get some tartan paint!

TAM SCOBBIE: Kevin McAllister was in charge of the Under-19s when he got one of the YTS boys Jason Watson to strip naked and sing 'Baa Baa Black Sheep'. Crunchie was getting him back as the young lad had been giving him stick. Luckily I've not had anything like that done to me.

GORDON RAE (Hibs stalwart): When I was manager at Gala Fairydean, we'd train outside in winter. We finished the session and I asked the boys to collect all the gear. One of the players, who didn't have the best eyesight, took off and started chasing what he thought was a ball. When he caught up with the white object it turned out to be a white Tesco bag.

BOBBY LINN: Dundee lost 6–2 in a youth game to Hibs and afterwards, our coach Kenny Cameron came in and gave us a piece of his mind. He was raging that much he ran and kicked a bag of balls – but one ball came loose and smacked a player in the face. Everyone was itching to laugh but we couldn't.

WILLIE KINNIBURGH: We were in Nico's bar in Glasgow with the Motherwell players when in walked this man with a black trench coat, black bowler hat and umbrella. Gerry Britton went over to him, grabbed his hat and umbrella and started performing his own version of Gene Kelly and 'Singin' in the Rain'. The guy was miffed and stormed out. Gerry had to go and chase him down to give him his hat and umbrella back.

CALLUM MACDONALD: We were on Peterhead's Christmas night out in Glasgow. On the way back we stopped off in Dundee for a day out, planning to get the last train to Aberdeen. We were all waiting on the platform when Stuart McKay decided he wanted a packet of crisps from the vending machine. The train arrived but Stuart was still not there. Then the train started to pull away. He was standing there on the platform, with his packet of crisps, with us all watching. And we had his bag. Stuart phoned Dougie Cameron, who was in Dundee, but he blanked his calls because he was with a young lady. He ended up staying in a Travelodge.

JAMIE MURPHY (Motherwell): We were going to training one day and some guy thought it would be smart to stop his van and shout out his window how rubbish we were. But he picked on the wrong team to do it to and he got absolutely abused by us. There were a few gestures made and he went away with his tail between his legs. He was really embarrassed because he didn't expect us to react.

STUART LOVELL (Hibs): The best abuse I heard was at Maine Road. We were heading off the pitch when some guy shouted: "You f*****g southern softy." I pointed out I was from Australia and he shouted back: "Still the f*****g south innit!"

DEREK ADAMS: When I moved to Burnley from Aberdeen, Ted McMinn was at the club. He wanted to move in with me down there, but he didn't in the end. He said to me if he was going to move in and I had any green plants, I'd better get rid of them.

Naked Truth

AVERT your eyes now! Footballers have no shame when it comes to showing off their bodies!

SCOTT MURRAY: I don't know if I should tell you this, but I do a thing when I'm drunk called −The Greyhound−. It's when I strip and tuck all my parts in between my legs behind me. At my mate's sister's birthday party the stripper never showed so I ended up doing it – and got £50 for it. I went all the way dancing to the song 'Male Stripper' by Man To Man, although I did use an ash-tray to hide my bits.

SCOTT MCLEAN: Part of my body looks like the nose of Gonzo from *The Muppet Show*. Everyone in the dressing room will know what I mean.

DAVID WINNIE: At KR Reykjavik, all the players gathered in a circle to psyche each other up before kick-off. Before my debut, the keeper Gulli Gunnleifsson, who was also a part-time stripper, told me all the new players had to touch his tattoo for luck. He took down his shorts and told me to touch one on a place I was never going to touch. He was serious and I didn't know what to say. And no, I didn't touch it.

MARK DOBIE (Gretna): At an end-of-season Gretna party, Craig Smart let off a fire extinguisher and was walking about naked in a maid's apron with a bottle of brown sauce in one hand and this extinguisher in the other.

GERRY COLLINS: John Lambie once brought in a girl to teach aerobics at Thistle. She told them it would make their muscles supple, so they were all doing their exercises and when she turned away every player pulled out their privates. She turned round and asked what they were doing and they said they were exercising another muscle. She didn't flinch and told them to tuck them away.

BRYAN GILFILLAN: Ross Tokely and Graeme Stewart had a great naked fight in the dressing room at Caley. Graeme stuck shampoo in Rosco's bag, so the big man threw Graeme's gear into the showers. But Graeme didn't take it too well and they started scrapping.

JOHN RANKIN (Ross County, Hibs): I was in Slovenia with Scotland Under-21s. We were all swimming but John Kennedy, Kris Boyd and Andy Dowie decided to whip off my shorts and throw them away so I was completely naked under the water. There was nothing I could do except make a periscope with my hand and come out the water to a standing ovation. The other people in the pool were not amused.

RYAN MCCANN: I wasn't long at Clyde when Stevie Masterton and Dougie Imrie had a naked stand-off. One had a bottle of ketchup and the other had a bottle of brown sauce and they just went for each other. The whole dressing room was covered in sauce and everyone was doubled up in stitches. They took it quite seriously.

DYLAN KERR: The funniest thing I've seen is a picture of Jim McIntyre with his d**k out at a Killie Christmas do. It wasn't a chipolata. Pat Nevin is standing next to him wearing a school uniform. Gary Holt and I dressed up as two tarts from the '50s with beehives, dresses and high heels.

NEIL OLIVER (Falkirk): Getting out the bath at Brockville used to be treacherous. John Hughes always sat at the steps and as you got out of the bath he'd grab you and bite your private parts. I think everyone in the Falkirk team had teethmarks down below. But it was just the big man's idea of good clean fun.

MICHAEL GARDYNE: On my first day at Morton, I walked into Cappielow and found Dean Keenan and Kieran McAnespie playing table tennis naked, apart from their boots and socks. I just thought, "Oh my God!" The disturbing thing was both of them were taking it so seriously.

DANNY INVINCIBILE (Kilmarnock): I've known John Maisano since we were nineteen and in the Under-20 Australian side and then I got to meet his brother Marco. As I was leaving Marconi they were arriving. I remember playing cards with them in Australia, we'd had a few sparkling mineral waters and decided the loser would do a dare. It ended up being me and they made me walk down a dual carriageway in just my underpants banging a wooden spoon on a saucepan. When I came to a set of lights, I had to cross the road and do an 'I'm a little tea pot' pose. People were in their cars thinking, "What the hell is this boy doing?"

ROBERT CONNOR: My tackle appeared on the front cover of the match programme of a Scottish Cup semi-final game between Aberdeen and Dundee United. It was a shot of a previous game between us and I was involved in a tussle for the ball with Paddy Connolly. The worst thing was I wasn't playing that day and was sitting in the stand while all the wives of the players could see me in my glory. You really have to look to see it, as it isn't so obvious.

JOHNNY WHELAN: At Hampden, the baths and showers are in separate bits. Stevie Reilly decided to slide in the shower completely naked and on his belly. He'd wave to us as he went past the door. He was red from head to toe.

JACK ROSS: Clyde's keeper Bryn Halliwell was known as 'The Exhibitionist' because before training and before games he likes to be naked in the dressing room – and he loves it. He shared a flat with Simon Mensing and they were like the guys out of *Dumb and Dumber* – they're not the brightest. Bryn stayed with me for a while, he's the most untidy and unhygienic person I know. I gave him clean sheets and a duvet but he didn't bother using them.

JOHN MAISANO: At Atalanta the players once grabbed the kit-man, stripped him naked and pinned him to the treatment table. They then taped up his whole body. No one else knew he was there. He was still taped up when we returned from training.

COLIN MILNE (Peterhead): We had an end-of-season party at Peterhead when *The Full Monty* song came on and I went all the way. My mum and dad were in the audience. My mum ran to the toilet in embarrassment while I covered my bits and pieces with a SHOE. It was great fun though and you should have seen the look on the faces of the two old ladies who were DJs.

STEVIE TOSH: After a few bevvies my mates stripped me naked and tied me to a wall just outside Stark's Park. They went away in the bus and left me stranded with only a pair of shoes on. I waited for ages stark naked before a taxi driver took pity on me.

CRAIG EASTON (Dundee United): I was in the canteen at Dundee United, holding my soup in one hand and a juice in the other. I was just walking past the dinner lady when Dave Bowman came in and pulled my trousers and pants down in front of her. She would have caught an eyeful if my bits and pieces hadn't been covered by a long t-shirt. But the worst part was I couldn't pull my trousers up until I sat down because my hands were full. I had to hobble back to my seat with my trousers at my ankles. I never did get Davie back for that because I knew if I did – the next time it would be even more embarrassing for me.

ANNE-MARIE BALLANTYNE: I was issuing tickets in the dressing room as I had no office at the time. Paul Ronald was in for a fitness test and he came in, stripped off and took his shower while I was doing the tickets. I kept my composure until I finished and left the dressing room and then I swear I went red from top to toe.

MIKE TEASDALE: When I was at Dundee, Roy McBain once ran stark naked round the greyhound track at Dens Park as a punishment for annoying the lads. He even started in the greyhound trap and did a whole lap. We were in stitches.

ERIK PAARTALU (Morton, Gretna): When I was fifteen, I was catching a few waves. I caught one all the way in and when I got closer to the shore there were two girls splashing about. I hadn't realised my boardies had slipped down my legs so when I stood up my family jewels were on parade.

STEVE LOVELL: When I was at Bournemouth, one lad let slip that it was his birthday so my brother and some other players decided to give him a birthday treat he wouldn't forget. They stripped him naked and dropped him off Bournemouth Pier in the middle of May. He was left to streak his way back to the club.

KENNY MILLER (Hibs, Celtic, Rangers, Scotland): There was a gay branch of the Hibs supporters' club and the story was that they came to games to see me. The tale came out just before an Edinburgh derby and I was expecting to get caned for it, but it wasn't too bad. The funny thing was that Yogi Hughes offered to wear all the black leather gear for their magazine if they gave us some money for the players' pool, but they declined his kind offer. I wonder why.

JOHN PAUL MCBRIDE: My good pal Stuart McCluskey tried to pull a fast one at St Johnstone. He was organising the Christmas night out, but the boys had put too much into the kitty. Stuart collected the money back from our managing director Stewart Duff. When the boys asked for the money we were told Stuart had it but he said the club still had it. He tried to pocket £120 so the lads stripped him naked and made him run two laps round McDiarmid Park with everyone watching.

ALAN MAYBURY: If it was your birthday at Leeds they would do things to you like make you run through the sprinklers with no clothes on. We made two of the younger players wrestle in cement on their birthday. It got to the stage where the cement was starting to set on them and it was difficult to get off.

DARREN YOUNG (Aberdeen, Dunfermline, Dundee): After a night of drinking, we went to a mate's house and were playing football naked in his back garden at 5.30 in the morning – we were all just wearing our shoes. Even more bizarrely, the neighbours invited us across to their party too.

PETER MACDONALD (St Johnstone): I ended up being shown nude on *TV's Naughtiest Blunders*. Simon Donnelly was being interviewed by Grampian TV at training when I decided to pull down my tracksuit trousers and pull my jersey over my face behind Simon. I never realised it was a woman who was doing the interview because she was wearing a tammy. I got asked by ITV if they could use it on their show and I didn't have a problem.

KEVIN FOTHERINGHAM: I thought it would be funny if I exposed myself for a couple of the Arbroath team pictures. About a month later it surfaced and I was told by the club they had printed 5,000 calendars with my bits hanging out. When I went to my work at the dockyards they had photocopied it all over the place.

COLIN NISH: Scott Thomson challenged me to a game of table tennis. The loser had to run round East End Park naked and of course I was beaten and had to do the forfeit. I lost a few times to Nipper – I never learned my lesson. I ran round the ground completely starkers with the whole team and manager watching.

MICHAEL MOORE: We went to Stockholm for Kevin Gaughan's stag do. Kevin is tee-total but he decided he was going to drink and he was the drunkest man in Stockholm. We tied him to a lamp-post in just his underwear and threw eggs at him.

COLIN CRAMB: There was a big chap at Doncaster called Darren Moore, who was about eighteen stone and the biggest centre half you have ever seen. We were coming out the showers when I got a bucket of dirty water and poured it over him. I had to run naked out the door, run across the car park, across a dual carriageway, on to Doncaster racecourse and jump some fences before I could get away from him. He was going to kill me and the manager had to make sure I didn't train with him until he calmed down.

JIMMY SANDISON: The crowd invaded the pitch as the final whistle blew after the last-ever game at Broomfield. Everyone made it into the dressing rooms in time except for one slowcoach – me. I was stripped naked apart from my knickers. That was only because I was holding on to them with both hands or it would have been really embarrassing. I eventually made it to the dressing room to roars of laughter from my team-mates.

MATT GLENNON (Falkirk, St Johnstone): Scott Sellars was dressed as Noddy and I was Big Ears on a Christmas night out at Bolton. I ended up wearing just the ears, my boxers and a pair of shoes. The lads decided to take items of clothing off me as we went from pub to pub. Unfortunately, it was hired – and I had to pay for it when I took it back to the shop.

KEVIN TINDAL: I was leaving Montrose and we were having a Christmas night out organised by Dave Larter when about five or six of the lads decided to strip to the 'Full Monty' in front of the

DJ. We stripped down to the boxers – but Colin McGlashan went all the way.

ALEX WILLIAMS: The Morton side that won the Third Division title went to Ibiza for four or five days. We were in a Scottish pub called Kilties. I ended up stripping naked and running outside. They locked the doors and I couldn't get in. The boys were at the window laughing at me.

RYAN MCGUFFIE: I was on trial at Rangers when I was fifteen and I was in the canteen getting my lunch. I had my tray in my hand when out of nowhere Ian Durrant whipped my shorts down to my ankles and I was left holding my tray showing off all my glory. I was mortified.

FRANK MCAVENNIE: I used to go to nightclubs Browns, Blondes and Stringfellows all in the same night. Blondes was owned by Georgie Best while Stringfellows looked after me for years. Strangely enough, the first time I went to Stringfellows I got a knockback because I was pretty p****d – now I've got life membership. Peter has been great with me and he gave me the club for the launch of my book. There have only been two book launches in there – his and mine.

GRAHAM BAYNE: When it was your birthday at Dundee, the lads would make you do something silly. I was made to run round Dens Park wearing nothing but steel toecap boots and a worker's helmet. I was egged on by the likes of Lee Wilkie and Jamie

Langfield. Another time I once went to the theatre not knowing it was a couple's night – and turned up on my own.

JOHN MACDONALD: We were on a trip with Rangers in the Middle East playing in Iraq and Jordan and it was quite boring so we would mess around the hotel. Ally McCoist and Cammy Fraser tied me down and stripped me to my underwear before sending me down to reception in the lift. As the door opened, there was a whole load of people about to get in until they saw me almost starkers lying on the floor.

CHRIS KILLEN: We were playing volleyball at my house with pals and the losing team had to do a naked run across the road and back. My pal and I lost. As we were crossing the busy road, my mate just put his head down and went for it. A car slammed on its brakes, skidded and missed him by inches. I could hardly look – I thought he was a goner.

DAVE BAIKIE: I was having a rant at the players after a game at Arbroath but while I was shouting at them I subconsciously started taking all my gear off and continued the rant stark naked.

STEPHEN SWIFT: During a Stranraer trip to Spain, David Graham was standing out on the balcony doing naked stretches in full view of everyone at the hotel. The boy has no shame.

SCOTT CHAPLAIN: Our nights out at Albion Rovers were always pretty mental because it was mostly young lads. One time we had our Christmas night in Newcastle and it resulted in a few of the boys running down the street completely naked. One of the boys nicked a busker's guitar and started singing.

TOM PARRATT: We had an Old Firm versus the rest of the world team match in training and the losers had to run around naked. David Winters was on the losing side and was starkers when he did a Klinsmann dive on the artificial surface. He didn't have much skin left.

ALEX RAE: I can't say who it was or what club it was at but one of the coaches at a party came into one of the rooms with a pair of underpants on his head and a towel wrapped around his waist. He showed us his party trick, which I can't mention in a family newspaper, and everyone just ran out the room.

DEAN HOLDEN: When you're an apprentice at Bolton, you go through an initiation where you are stripped naked, have to stand on a table and sing a song. But before you sing they turn out the lights, beat you up, smear you with Vaseline, cover you in boot polish and stick you in an ice bath. I sang 'Football's Coming Home'. Three of the Irish lads stood up and sang a Boyzone song. I seem to remember it was the Scottish contingent of Owen Coyle, John McGinlay and Stephen McAnespie who were behind it.

ALEX KEDDIE: The Ross County dressing room is a strange place when Paul Lawson decides to walk around naked. He is no stranger to a cheeseburger or a fish supper. He actually thinks he's a sex god.

MARC TWADDLE: The Partick boys were in Lineker's Bar when Willie Kinniburgh went off and was away for ages. We were wondering where he was when he walked past hundreds of people completely naked and started dancing round the poles.

PAUL KINNAIRD: I never wore a jockstrap, but I soon changed that after a game at Ayr. I tussled at the corner flag with a defender who pulled my shorts down and to the side. Everyone saw what I had to offer – admittedly, not that much.

MURRAY DAVIDSON: A youngster at Livingston and Martin Scott had to run round the park naked during a thunderstorm to get his Christmas tips from the senior players. Luckily I didn't have to do it. David McNamee and Stuart Lovell were behind it.

CRAIG MCKEOWN: When I was a kid at Dunfermline, Gary Greenhill decided to do a naked slide in the dressing room. He lathered himself up with soap, dived on to the floor and slid towards the door. He timed it to perfection because Billy Kirkwood walked in and was taken right out.

ROSS FORBES (Motherwell): When I was on work experience on my last day at Motherwell, the older boys in the team grabbed me in the showers and covered me in black boot polish from head to toe. They then put me outside on the pitch with absolutely no clothes on and locked me out. I think a few people were out on the pitch and, as a fifteen-year-old, I was pretty embarrassed.

JAMES MCPAKE (Livingston, Coventry): Mark Proctor told us to have a day out one Sunday when he was Livi manager. We were in the Sports Bar in Sauchiehall Street and as I walked back from the toilet, one of our players was sitting on the couch with nothing on, just drinking his beer. I'm surprised no one phoned the police!

Red-Faced

THEY can be sensitive souls, our footballers, and here is a list of embarrassing moments for some that have left them with egg on their face.

RAB MCKINNON: Tam Cowan once got hold of a picture of Celtic's Stuart Slater grabbing my shorts, exposing my tackle. It was a cold January day and wasn't impressive. He had a competition on his radio show to win a picture of me and a packet of ginger nuts.

PAUL MCGRILLEN: I was on a night out with Brian Hamilton, Ally Graham, Derek Ferguson and Graham Mitchell. Brian invited us back to his place and when we got to the house I walked in on his missus while she was breast-feeding their kid. I went a bit scarlet. The rest of them laughed at me.

TAM MCMANUS: I was staying in the same hotel as Paul Gascoigne while I was at Boston United and he sent me some flowers and chocolates saying it was from the wee bird at reception that I really fancied. I was buzzing and went down to say thanks and ask her out. I got a big custard pie and went scarlet red when she said she had a fella.

KEVIN DRINKELL: When I was introduced to the Rangers players, Ian Durrant quipped: "F**k me, they've signed Chi Chi the Panda!" Some of the guys still call me that.

TOM STEVEN: I once chatted up a transvestite in a club, although I never realised 'she' was a bloke. I went into a club not knowing that it was a bar for transvestites. I was chatting her up, but when I went to kiss her I could feel 'her' stubble. I couldn't believe it was a guy and he just said, "I must be looking good tonight."

PAUL DEVLIN: I have followed through in training before, but in one game for Birmingham against Norwich City I could barely run because I had a bad case of diarrhoea. I couldn't run because if I did people would have seen it as I was wearing white shorts! I had to wait until half time and I think everyone in the dressing room heard me when I finally got to the toilet.

COLIN STEWART: I wasn't long into my relationship with Julie Fleeting when her dad Jim walked into his en-suite bathroom while I was sitting on the toilet with my trousers round my ankles, reading a paper. I was so embarrassed it took me an hour to go downstairs. Jim still brings it up occasionally.

KEITH WRIGHT (Hibs legend): While we were away with Hibs I'd the job of keeping all the players' passports. I was in the toilet at the airport when someone reached under the door and stole my rucksack. I ran out into the lounge chasing the guy with my trousers still round my ankles. It was Kevin McAllister.

LIAM BUCHANAN: I had to tell the manager that I would be out for two weeks because I had an in-growing hair in my bum that required an operation. It was really painful. I was put to sleep for the surgery. The boys found out and I got a lot of stick for it but it was sore like you wouldn't believe.

STEVEN CRAIG: I was in St Ives when I was about fifteen or sixteen with a mate when we started chatting to a couple of girls. The one I was speaking to kept going "Eh, eh, eh?" to everything I was saying so I asked her if she was deaf. Then I spotted she had two hearing aids as she flicked her hair. That was pretty embarrassing so I just walked away.

GERRY COLLINS: There was a small social club at Hamilton and they challenged the players to a singing contest. Somebody came up with the idea that it was a fancy dress party as well. I went as Al Jolson with the black make-up, the black suit, the white shirt and the white gloves but when I arrived no one was dressed up. The whole place fell silent and then burst into laughter.

STEVE PATERSON: I literally was left red-faced when I stayed with a Japanese friend for five days on an island in 1984. On the first day, I went down to the beach and fell asleep and I woke up three hours later covered in blisters and was red raw. I ended up going to the hospital with sunstroke and a very red face.

JIM CHAPMAN (Albion Rovers, Dumbarton): I ripped my shorts in a game for Albion Rovers in the 1980s and ran to the side of the pitch to quickly change them. But I fell over and there was my bare backside sticking up in the air. Everyone started laughing and all I could hear was: "There's a full moon," and "He's made an a**e of that." Luckily there were only about fifty fans and a dog there.

RONNIE MACDONALD: Bryn Halliwell was at Clyde on trial and in training I had a little game of penalties with him. I tucked my suit trousers into my shoes and he let the first couple past him. Then at 4-0, he started to get very agitated. I took out a cigar, lit it and scored another. Then I went on my mobile phone and spoke to someone and scored a few more. It got to 10-0 and everyone chanted "Granny! Granny!" at him. He's never lived it down.

STEVEN THOMPSON: I had been out on the Saturday night and got home before my folks to see the back door ajar. I sprinted out the house and phoned all my mates. Five of them came round with golf clubs, baseball bats, you name it. There was no way I was facing this alone. Turns out my mum had left the door open to let the dog in.

GLYNN HURST: When I was on holiday in Greece with my brother, a woman came up to us and started trying to chat us up. We couldn't really be bothered with her and started trying to wind her up. She asked what I did for a living and I told her I was at Cambridge University studying to be a florist! She fell for it and started talking to me about flowers – I had to pretend I knew something to keep the joke going.

MARK REYNOLDS (Motherwell): The first-team at Motherwell would pay for the YTS boys to go away on a day trip, such as paintballing or go-karting, as a bonus. But to get it, we would have to put on a show at the Christmas lunch and we'd have to dress up. The first year we had to sing 'Lady Marmalade' dressed as French maids and cheerleaders. We had to sing it in front of everyone at Fir Park – the first-team, staff, coaches, cleaners and Terry Butcher. The next year we were Take That, looking pure camp. I'm not really one for acting but you had to do it. A few boys have died on that stage and it can make or break you up there.

JULIE FLEETING (Scotland's top woman scorer): I was with the Scotland team and we were flying out of Gatwick Airport to travel to Portugal for a tournament. The England team were also leaving at the same time and they always get more expense money than us and have all the latest gadgets. A girl in our team, who'll remain nameless, sneaked up behind one of the English girls while she was talking to someone on her mobile. She pulled the girl's tracksuit trousers down and she didn't know what to do because she had one hand on her phone. She just stood there with her trousers at her ankles.

JAMES GRADY (Dundee, Ayr, Gretna, Dundee United): I remember one Valentine's Day my missus Emma asked me to go to a shop in Glasgow called 'Heaven and Hell' and buy her something nice. I went after training with Dundee. Eddie Annand and Barry Smith came along. I got a bit embarrassed when we went into the shop and ended up picking up the first bra and knickers set I saw. When I got it to the counter, the woman told me it cost £145. The lads were howling with laughter but I couldn't back out. So my credit card was hit hard. The worst thing was that they didn't fit and Emma had to take them back.

SCOTT MCLEAN: An ex of mine walked in on me while I was in bed with another girl. She took my stereo and threw it at my head and chucked the other girl out of my flat. We had a heart-to-heart and then we split up. It was a terrible thing to do and I am more ashamed of it than embarrassed.

STUART MCCAFFREY: When I was at Hibs, I was arrested for having a can of Irn Bru in my possession whilst sitting in the stand. I had my club suit on but I was still taken out the ground, past my dad and sister in the stand and charged with having a controlled container. Fortunately Douglas Cromb, our chairman at the time, got the charges dropped and spared my blushes. What made it even more embarrassing was that it was the first time I had been in the actual squad to face Celtic.

JERRY O'DRISCOLL: I was buying some things for my new house and had to supply my details. But when I told the guy who I was he revealed his son kept talking about a footballer with the same name who'd p****d his career away at Dundee and was a total waster. I just kept my head down.

TONY BULLOCK: I was actually on stage with the hypnotist Paul McKenna at a show in Manchester. I was one of his victims and he made me think I was a chicken and also made me chat up a sixteen-stone man thinking it was my girlfriend. I knew what I was doing but couldn't stop myself from doing it.

COLIN MCMENAMIN: My cousin Siean embarrassed me in front of Ant and Dec. They are big Newcastle fans and were at the ground when Siean asked them to sign a few things. They said no problem and shook his hand. Then he just told them: "You have no talent whatsoever," and walked out the door. I just cringed. He thinks he's a legend for doing that.

RAB MCKINNON: We were away with Motherwell on a pre-season tour in Middlesbrough and a guy in a pub said: "I know you, you're famous." I was well chuffed that a Well fan should be that far south – then he said: "You're Butch Dingle from Emmerdale Farm." I was gutted but I eventually saw the soap opera and I have to admit he had a point – the nickname 'Butch' has stuck to this day.

CRAIG MCEWAN: I was about seventeen and there was this girl I wanted to impress. I thought I would show off and prove how athletic I was, so decided to sprint in front of her but I tripped on the kerb and fell flat on the pavement. Needless to say, I didn't get a date.

MICKY WEIR: Archie Macpherson was commentating on me for the first time and said I should be getting messages for my mum on a Saturday. That stuck with me and I got slagged for it. I've never met Archie to thank him.

KENNY CLARK: I was chosen to do an Old Firm game and my son Scott asked why it wasn't "Scotland's top whistler Hugh Dallas". He didn't get any pocket money that week.

MARTYN CORRIGAN: When I was a YTS boy at Falkirk, Yogi Hughes and Ian McCall made me walk across the dressing room like a puppet from *Thunderbirds*. I had to nod my head and raise my hands otherwise they would give me a doing. They did it for their own amusement. I could have taken one of them on but not both.

SCOTT MCKENZIE (Falkirk, St Mirren): I was called in at the last minute to replace Tony Parks at a charity dinner at the Thistle Hotel in Glasgow. It was attended by over 400 top businessmen and there was a personality on each table, including Gordon Sherry and Richard Gough. No one at my table knew who I was – I didn't expect them to – and it was made worse when compere Emlyn Hughes introduced all the 'personalities'. We had to stand up and give a wee wave and I was introduced as Tony Parks in front of all these people. Ouch!

KENNY ARTHUR: I started working in Morgan Stanley bank and obviously it is different clothes in that environment compared to football. I came in to training in the morning wearing a pink checked shirt which was what I would wear at work in the bank later in the afternoon. I hung it up in the dressing room but when I came back the lads were sitting at a table using it as a tablecloth.

COLIN STEWART: My brother Ross was giving a speech at my wedding last year when he asked everyone to turn their chairs to face one direction. A big TV screen came down and Ross said they were going to show all my greatest saves on video. A few minutes went by and nothing came on the screen and Ross just said: "We all know Colin hasn't made any great saves."

GARY DEMPSEY: When we were kids at Everton, we used to dive into the first-team's bath after training. On one occasion, the caretaker came in and told us to get out as there was bleach in the bath. Now that was painful.

JIM BETT: We were about to play Australia in the play-off match at Hampden for the 1986 World Cup. I didn't read the itinerary properly and turned up at the wrong hotel – which just happened to be where the Australians were staying. I walked in and said I was Jim Bett with Scotland and they looked at me funny, as did some of the Australians who were sitting in the lobby.

WILLIE KINNIBURGH: My girlfriend Paula had given birth to our baby boy Rian. I went out the following day and had a heavy night. The next day I went to the hospital to see them but I ended up collapsing and next thing I woke up with six nurses around me. The whole few days got to me and I ended up in the bed next to my girlfriend. When all the visitors came in they were wondering what on earth I was doing there.

STEVIE MURRAY: I got the hook at half time in a game against Dundee United at Rugby Park. It was embarrassing because in the match ratings in *SunSport*, the reporter Robert Grieve said I'd have been better off playing on the swings with my pals. All the lads slagged me off for it and stuck it up on the dressing room wall. It still gets brought up. To be fair, I did have a disaster.

JIM BALLANTYNE: My wife Gillian and I received an un-expected visitor in the office – the cleaner. I don't need to explain further do I?

PAUL SHEERIN: I had a heavy summer drinking Guinness and I put on two stone before I went to pre-season at Ayr United. Gordon Dalziel said he was happy with everyone apart from me. He said: "The fat b*****d in the corner – you've got a lot of work to do!" I got a hard time for that.

MARC TWADDLE: At Falkirk, we had a big do with the sponsors called the Falkirk Oscars. Each player would have to go down a catwalk when their name was called out and you'd have a theme song played. Just as I was about to be called up I could see some of the boys sniggering and knew something was up. Yogi had dubbed me Rodney Trotter and when I started walking down the theme to *Only Fools and Horses* was played. All the lads started shouting: "Alright Dave!"

GARY MCDONALD: At Kilmarnock, one of the YTS boys Chris Boyle and I wanted extra cash so we decided to clean cars for a fiver. We got two customers – Bobby Williamson and Gerry McCabe – and we started washing their cars with a mop. But we scratched Gerry's bonnet and he wasn't in the best of moods. We didn't get paid and it was the end of our car washing business.

TAM SCOBBIE: One New Year, all the family came round and one of my younger cousins went and chose a DVD for us all to watch. Let's just say it wasn't a PG DVD – I got some stare from my granddad.

GERRY MCCABE: Archie Macpherson was raving about me during a game against Aberdeen in the Tennent's Sixes. But then I missed from a yard out – and after that I was known as Gerry Macpherson.

PAUL BURNS: The night before the Scottish Cup semi-final when we beat Aberdeen, we were sitting down for dinner at the hotel when a waitress brought over a gift bag. I opened it up and it contained a nappy, baby pants and a note signed from my girl-friend telling me to have a good night's sleep and not to worry. I found out it was the quiet assassin Jamie McQuilken who stitched me up.

14

Stitch Up

YOU never think it can happen to you – but no one is immune from a prank. Even the street savvy players can fall victim.

JIMMY SANDISON: I was driving home from Airdrie with John Martin, Evan Balfour, Graham Harvey and John Watson in our clapped out Mazda 626, which we all owned. John Watson found the central locking system was broken and we couldn't open the doors. He decided to leave by the window which was a big mistake because as he got halfway out with his legs still inside, we raised the window and trapped him, whipped his tracksuit bottoms down, then pushed him out the window and left him in the Maybury car park with his trousers at his ankles.

SCOTT HIGGINS: I bet one of our players at Queensland that he couldn't hide a ten-cent piece on his body without me finding it. The boys chipped in five dollars each for a fifty-dollar kitty which he'd win if I couldn't find it. We were in a pub and I went outside and smeared my fingers over an exhaust pipe. When I started looking for the coin on him his face, ears and neck were covered in black oil. He didn't realise for ages that his face was totally black.

MARK REYNOLDS: When you first go in as a YTS boy at Motherwell, the older boys initiate you in the changing room. I got tied up and hosed down naked outside. Another guy, John Paul Grant, gave a bit of lip so they tied his hands and feet behind his back, boot-polished his face and body, Vaselined his hair, put Deep Heat in the private parts then stuck him in a boot hamper and left him in the corridor so folk could walk by and have a peek.

PETER HETHERSTON: At Raith Rovers, the boys sent me a letter saying they wanted me to appear in an episode of *Taggart*. It said they liked my rough voice and were offering me £600 for appearing and £900 for doing a nude scene. I was told to turn up at Firhill but I got wind of it when I overheard Gordon Dalziel and Ronnie Coyle in the toilet and knew something was up.

STEWART HILLIS: When Andy Roxburgh was national boss, he asked Andy Cameron to come and entertain the boys to relax them before a game. But the players decided to play a joke by not laughing at any of Andy's jokes. The only person laughing was Roxburgh, who wasn't in on the joke. So there is Andy dying a death until fifteen minutes in when he caught on and said: "Ya shower of b*****ds!"

DAVID GRAHAM: One of my mates put the phone number of another mate in the free ads with "For sale: Three-piece leather suite, brand-new, reason for sale: moving abroad, £250". My mate was getting crazy amounts of phone calls every day because it was such a good deal.

MARCO RUITENBEEK (Dunfermline): When I was in Holland with Go Ahead Eagles one player had his boots filled with water and stuck in the freezer. It was hilarious because he was looking for them and couldn't find them anywhere. Eventually he found them frozen solid but he saw the funny side to it.

IAN WILSON: Kevin Sheedy still doesn't know that when we were flying somewhere we would put loads of salt into his meals and he would always complain to the cabin crew. We also used to stick Vodka into his orange juice.

ANDY MCLAREN: Mo Johnston and Ally McCoist played a funny prank on Freddie Van der Hoorn when Dundee United played Rangers at Ibrox. We were making a substitution and when the boards were held up they told Freddie he was the one to go off – of course he wasn't but Freddie didn't realise until he had trotted to the side of the pitch. McCoist and Johnston were laughing away. I have to confess to a prank I played at Kilmarnock's pre-season training camp in Italy on Kris Boyd and Gary McDonald. They threw water balloons at Stevie Fulton so I sneaked into their room and put shaving foam all over their bags and beds.

MARK DOBIE: Keith Houchen set up an absolute cracker at Hartlepool one day. There was one player who was always bragging about the women he was with and once said he had picked up a girl in the red light district. So Keith got one of his mates to come up to the ground, pretending he was a policeman, to question this lad. He was standing there absolutely terrified and it was hilarious. We eventually let him in on it, but not before dragging it out for a while.

DAVID WINNIE: At Ayr we had a guy called Stevie Welsh who was a right nutter. We were staying in a hotel in Troon one day and he took Glynn Hurst's car keys and parked his car in the middle of a huge puddle. It had been raining all night and by the morning the car park had turned into a lake. All you could see was the roof of his car. He couldn't get in it.

HARRY CAIRNEY: My wife Lorna got me a good one on April Fool's day when she phoned me up and pretended to be a viewer for the house we were selling. I ended up cleaning everything before Lorna decided to tell me it was her. I was so angry.

SCOTT THOMSON: John Potter was a player at Dunfermline who always thought he was a bit of a looker so Jason Dair, Stevie Crawford and I decided to phone him up and pretend to be a modelling agency. We told him we wanted him to model balaclavas and socks. He ended up telling the boys he was being paid £500 to model clothes before he eventually came clean that it was socks. We waited a week before telling him it was a joke.

CAMPBELL MONEY: When I was first called up for Scotland Jock Stein told me I was rooming with Kenny Dalglish. I pretty much s**t myself. That night someone claiming to be a reporter phoned up asking me what it was like to room with Kenny but it turned out to be that b*****d Alan Hansen.

SCOTT MURRAY: Our coach Leroy Rosenior had taken the ball bags out of the big sack so I decided I would hide in it. When the coach came to get more balls I jumped out and scared him – it's the first time I've ever seen a black man go white. He was laughing about it afterwards though.

GED BRANNAN: We were drinking with the Tranmere boys in a Dublin pub when Shaun Garnett went to the toilet. Liam O'Brien – who knew some of the locals – then sent some of the guys into the toilet after him and they pretended they were the IRA. They stripped him and when he came out he was only in his boxers – and petrified. But when he saw us laughing he took it in good spirit.

CALLUM MACDONALD: Dougie Cameron and Chris Brash got me at my twenty-first birthday party. We were staying at a hotel but they managed to convince the front desk to give them my keys. They kidded them on they had a surprise present and wanted to leave it in the room. They basically turned it upside down, cut up my clothes and bed sheets and put some flowers from the hotel in the room. When I walked in I thought how nice it was of the hotel to leave me flowers but as it wasn't long before I saw the carnage.

I think Chris Hegarty might have been involved too — those two definitely were.

STEVIE MILNE: I got a phone call the day before April Fool's from a girl saying she was from *SunSport* wanting to do a story and take my picture. I was top league scorer in Scotland at the time at Forfar. I was a bit suspicious, but went to Station Park and sure enough she was there. She had a football boot spray-painted gold. I held it up, but as my photo was being taken, Ralph Brand snuck up behind me with a bit of paper saying "April Fool". The photo's on the wall at the ground.

DICK CAMPBELL: There was a Raith Rovers fan in Kirkcaldy who had his house and garden draped in team colours right down to his garden gnomes. He was in the paper because the council had deemed it an eyesore and wanted him to tone it down. The producers of *Beadle's About* thought it'd be funny to get me and a couple of Dunfermline players along to shock him just as he came in from work. So Andy Tod, Hamish French and I dressed up in workie gear and started taking gnomes and stuff out of his garden. He approached us and said: "What the hell are you doing?" Then in came Jeremy and said: "Here's a couple of your favourite people!"

MICHAEL STEWART (Man. United, Hearts): Manchester United physio David Fevre tells a great story of when he was on his stag do, how his pals got him blotto with booze and put a stookie on him when he conked out. They then brought some old X-ray scans and told him he'd broken his leg. He got married later that day with the stookie in every picture. He went on honeymoon and it was only when he got back they had the heart to tell him his leg wasn't broken.

BRIAN MCPHEE: A strange package arrived at Livingston addressed to Marino Keith. He opened it in front of the rest of the lads and a bundle of hair fell out of the envelope. There was a wee note saying: "I notice you have been going a bit thin on top recently – this may help you." It turned out to be Gerry Britton's hair and it's just as well, because he badly needed a haircut.

JAMIE MCALLISTER: Kevin Rutkiewicz and David Preece went out and bought the most tasteless wallpaper they could find and proceeded to cover David Lilley's car in it. It was a class decorating act, all kept on with Sellotape! Lilley wasn't too pleased, but then he has pulled off a few wind-ups himself – live by the sword die by the sword.

KEVIN MCDONALD: The physio at Airdrie, Mick, didn't know the boys let down the same tyre of his car every day. He would keep blowing it up every day and telling us how he had got a slow puncture. He eventually forked out for a brand new tyre even though there was nothing wrong it. He will know now reading this.

ROSS MCCORMACK (Rangers, Motherwell): Brian McLean bought a new Lexus. He didn't really want to drive it to training because in the winter it gets a bit muddy. So he went down in the young boys' bus and left his car at the club. We got the keys, which he had left in his trousers in the changing room, and stuffed all the empty bottles in his car then emptied a bin or two in there. He had to send it back to Lexus to get the seats sorted out. He was raging.

ROBERT SNODGRASS: There was a keeper who played at Livi called Scott Findlay. I realised how gullible he was so me and Scott McLaughlin phoned him up and kidded on we were boxing promoters. We told him we could set him up with a meeting to get inspirational speeches off Frank Bruno and Sugar Ray Leonard. We kept him going for two days but we had to tell him it was a wind-up because he was all set to drive down from Perth to Glasgow to meet them.

CHARLIE ADAM (Rangers, St Mirren, Ross County, Blackpool): At St Mirren, the boys wound me up a beauty at the end of the season. I got a letter through the post from the SPFA saying that I was nominated as Young Player of the Year. I had to phone a number and tell them I would be attending the dinner. I was really chuffed with myself, really pleased. But about a week later Iain Anderson said Ian Maxwell and John Potter were just winding me up. I was raging and it's only now I see the funny side. But it turned out that everyone at the club was in on it – even the gaffer Gus MacPherson.

CHRIS SWAILES: The Rotherham chairman's secretary took a phone call from who she thought was the Ipswich chairman David Sheepshanks to ask for permission to interview Ronnie Moore for the job. She told Ronnie and he started talking about it in the media saying he had taken Rotherham as far as he could and would like the Ipswich job. But it wasn't Sheepshanks who phoned and it was someone doing a wind-up.

GILLIAN DONALDSON: It was the middle of winter and our groundsman at Cappielow was trying to determine what the surface temperature of the pitch was and whether to put the covers down or not. He didn't just buy a thermometer. Instead, he decided to stick two glasses of water on the pitch to see if they would freeze. But Andy Bryan and Stevie Frail thought it would be hysterically funny if they got ice cubes from the ice machine and put them in the glasses. The poor groundsman went outside and couldn't understand why there were ice cubes in the glasses. They fobbed him off with theories about ground temperature and its effects.

JAMIE MCKENZIE: Lawrie Ellis had a little Mini Metro car and loved it. On his nineteenth birthday, one of the lads got hold of some police tape so we wrapped his entire car up in it and you could hardly see a bit of it. He wasn't best pleased – especially since it took him ages to peel the tape off.

BRIAN HAMILTON (Hibs, Hearts, St Mirren): Andy Goram used to do a classic trick on all the new lads at Easter Road. He would bet them a couple of quid they couldn't hide a five-pence piece in any part of their upper body. They could hide it in their ears, their hair – anywhere they liked. Andy would then go out and run his hands on an exhaust to get soot on his hands and come back in, rub his hands over the victim's face until they were covered in soot, then tell them they'd won the bet.

NEIL OLIVER: Kevin McAllister once had me believing Kevin Keegan wanted to sign me for Newcastle. I was on holiday with the Falkirk lads in Magaluf and he said his wife told him the papers back home said Keegan has been watching me and was ready to make a bid. I tried not to look interested, but was really excited. The thing was, the lads from Raith Rovers and Airdrie were there too and Crunchie had them in on the joke too. They all came up to me and wished me all the best. Eventually I went away and phoned my wife Lynn, but she hadn't heard anything so I told her to buy all the papers every day. It wasn't until I got back home I found out it was a huge wind-up. I was gutted.

SCOTT MCLEAN: Gerry Collins got me at an awards ceremony when I won the Second Division Player of the Year. He got someone to come up and pretend he wanted to give me a boot deal with Adidas and I'd get loads of free gear. Weeks later, I was still asking Gerry when I was getting my stuff.

JOHN PAUL MCBRIDE: We were supposed to have a night out with a bad gear theme. It was to be on the Sunday after our game with Dundee United but was postponed and rescheduled for the Tuesday. Andy Gibson was on loan at Stirling Albion at the time but we never told him it had been cancelled. He was phoning asking where we were and Gerry Britton had him running around Glasgow. It wasn't until 10pm he found out everyone was at home.

DARREN YOUNG: We were staying at Dunblane Hydro with Aberdeen and were having a night out. Dean Windass and Mike Newell came back early, barged into Jim Leighton's room and attacked him with a fire extinguisher. Twenty minutes later, when Derek Stillie and I came in, Jim grabbed me by the throat, pinned me to the wall and threatened to kick the s**t out of me. He thought it had been me but Derek was trying to tell him it wasn't and that we'd only just arrived. He eventually calmed down.

STEVEN CRAIG: At Raith Rovers, Jimmy Nicholl once bet Jay Stein he could run round the pitch quicker than he could drink a pint of water. Jay accepted the challenge and Alex Smith came out with a pint of boiling water. You never take on Jimmy. He told Zander Diamond he would race him for a tenner – what he didn't say was whoever won would pay the £10 so Zander had to cough up.

IAN CAMPBELL: I remember once John Ritchie had the pockets of his jacket filled with snow. I came in and he went mental. He ended up tying everyone's trousers in a knot and was throwing them out on the park.

MICHAEL MOORE: I was in Ayia Napa with Stephen Swift. I put a milk carton under his bed. It went off straight away but

Stephen had no idea what it was. We were there for six nights and it smelt bad but it wasn't until the last day he found it.

MARTIN BAVIDGE (Caley Thistle, Forfar, Peterhead): We set up Stuart McCaffrey at Caley. He came back from holiday where he had met a girl. He got her number but we changed it so that when we texted him he thought it was her. We arranged to meet him one night and he got showered, shaved and dressed up to meet her. A group of us went in a car opposite to where he was meeting her. He stood there for twenty minutes before we felt sorry for him and told him. He took it fairly well.

GORDON MCQUEEN: We were in Tel Aviv with Manchester United when a group of us put a dead turtle that had washed up on the beach into a hotel worker's bath. It was a massive thing. We got into trouble because it stank the hotel out.

ALAN ROUGH: Before a friendly between Hibs and Dinamo Kiev, Gordon Hunter came in wearing a pair of black leather trousers and thought he was really groovy. He was a sub that night and helped me to warm up. It was pouring with rain and the pitch was a bog. I told him to take shots in at me and I was flying all over the place into the mud. When we finished Gordon looked at me and said: "Are those my leather trousers?" I put them on instead of my trackie bottoms.

MARTYN CORRIGAN: There was a kid at Motherwell called John Connolly and Stevie Nicholas and I took the registration plates of his car off and put them on upside down. He didn't know anything about it until the police pulled him up for it.

BILLY KIRKWOOD: I was selling my house and Ralph Milne phoned up, put on a voice and said he was interested. I tidied up the house frantically but the next day Ralph put on his voice in the dressing room and I was raging.

DANNY CUNNING: Someone at the club stole my brown shoes and I started getting postcards from all over the world with messages. I got one with a pair of shoes wearing a London police hat. The message read: "I tried to visit the Queen today but they wouldn't let me in with these shoes!" I think it was our security man Tom Purdie. He collects little trinkets from police forces and even has an FBI wallet. I've had postcards from Greece, France, Lithuania, America and even Singapore. All the clues point to Tam. He denied it though.

ANDY DOWIE: I got a text from Alex Keddie saying: "I need a jobby!" It turned out Michael Gardyne had stolen his phone and texted everyone the same message.

JOHN MACDONALD: If we were staying in a hotel, Ally McCoist would get messages to the players rooms saying they had to be up at 7am for breakfast and training. All the players would turn up first thing and of course Ally would still be in his bed. We kicked the s**t out of him for that.

JIM BALLANTYNE: We played a prank on Bryan Prunty when he had two games left to score one goal and get his bonus. We wrote a letter saying he was being internally disciplined and would miss the last two games. He did play in the next game and scored – then directed some abuse to me in the directors' box.

WILLIE KINNIBURGH: Ian Maxwell sewed the sleeves on my jumper together. I had a Scotland top on one day and Craig Hinchcliffe signed it "Best Wishes, Mark Roberts". At Motherwell, Gerry Britton nailed my Predator boots to the wall. If I dish it out I have to take it.

STEPHEN DOBBIE: When I was at St Johnstone, but out on loan at Dumbarton, the boys arranged a fancy dress night for Halloween. I took my costume to training that night and afterwards made my way into town dressed as Austin Powers. When I arrived in Campus all the boys where sitting in their normal gear and there was me dressed as Powers! Great practical joke – even if it was on me.

ROBBIE RAESIDE: When I was at Raith Rovers the whole club was in on a wind-up, including the office staff. They gave all the players lottery tickets to win a car and sent me an official letter saying I had won. I fell for it. I suspect it was Gordon Dalziel or Ally Graham who came up with it.

ARTHUR NUMAN: At my first club Haarlem, most of us had jobs in the morning and would then train in the afternoon. One of the players worked in an abattoir and brought in a cow's head and put it in another player's bag. When he opened the bag it was hilarious – it's the only time I've ever seen a coloured man turn pale. He was shaking for about ten minutes and was shouting it was voodoo.

TAM FORSYTH (Motherwell, Rangers): I played with Dixie Deans at Motherwell and he was a right one for the dressing-room antics. I had just passed my driving test and I was sitting at lights in Motherwell when Dixie ran up to my car out of nowhere, tapped on the window and when I rolled it down he stole my keys out of the ignition.

ROSS CAMPBELL (Forfar): When I was a student in Edinburgh I lived in digs. The doorbell kept going one morning. It turned out one of my pals placed an ad in a paper saying I had three Golden Labrador puppies to give away. There were about thirty people there.

GARY ARBUCKLE: Kenny Brannigan used to cycle in to training at Glasgow Green with Queen of the South. The bike was his pride and joy and he was always going on about how he paid over a grand for it. So when he was setting up training, we took his tyres off, hid them, then wrapped up the bike in bandages and put it on a stretcher. He wasn't best pleased. Michael McGowan and Scott Robertson were behind it.

15

Toilet Humour

PLAYERS can't stop baring their bits. They are obsessed. And when you need to go, you need to go . . .

ALEX WILLIAMS: The best ever headline about me was "Keepy Uppy King!" It was a match report of a Morton game that Bill Leckie wrote for *The Sun*. He picked up on an interview I did for the match programme which asked me what I had in my pocket – money, keys, my mobile and Viagra. It appeared as a full page in *The Sun*.

LEE MAIR: There are three baths in the dressing room at Dens Park and after training they were made ready for the coaches Stevie Campbell, Ray Farningham and Paul Mathers. One time Lee Wilkie decided to take a dump in Paul's bath and it was hidden by the bubbles, although one of the kids told Paul about it before he got in it.

STEVE PATERSON: When I was younger we used to have a competition in the winter to see who could bare their bottom to a fire the longest. I still hold the record with twelve seconds.

ANDY DOWIE: Stuart Anderson was once left a little present in his sock after training. Stuart was about to put the sock on when he smelled something funny. He wasn't amused. I won't name the culprit.

BOBBY LINN: The Morton boys were on a night out in Glasgow and when we got to George Square, Dean Keenan and Michael Gardyne decided they needed the toilet, so they pulled down their trousers and underwear and peed on the daffodils. Everyone was watching so I walked away as if I didn't even know them.

ADAM COAKLEY: When I was younger at Motherwell, the older players were putting the younger players' heads into an ice bucket. I didn't realise before it was my turn that the boys had peed in it. I am sure Marc Fitzpatrick was involved. I stuck my head halfway in before suddenly realising.

BRIAN MCPHEE: I went to the Neil Diamond concert with my mother-in-law. We had a great time and there's no way I regretted going to see him – it's what happened afterwards that I regret. I went out to Victoria's, had a few beers and made my way back to my mother-in-law's house and for some reason decided to do a wee wee all over the floor. I left a big puddle but didn't know about it until the morning. I had to hide in my room.

JOHN MCVEIGH: We were up at the Old Course Hotel in St Andrews after filming *A Shot at Glory* and were all having a drink. About half past eleven, Bobby Duvall says he is off to bed and Big John Martin stands up in the middle of the hotel and stutters: "B-B-Bobby is that y-y-you goin' upstairs for a w**k?" I couldn't believe he had said that to this Hollywood legend. The whole place just erupted and Bobby laughed and gave him a finger.

PAUL MCHALE: I got flung out of a pub a couple of days before my wedding. We were playing a drinking game and one of the forfeits if you lost was to go to the toilets and pee with your trousers and boxers round your ankles. Just as I was doing it, a bouncer walked in and chucked me out. I couldn't really complain about it.

LIAM BUCHANAN: Darren McGregor is always doing silly things. He walked in on Marc Millar while he was sitting on the toilet and asked him if he could watch. I'm hoping he was joking.

STEVE BOWEY: I used to wet my bed until I was fourteen. I used to get so embarrassed but now I just find it funny. It doesn't bother me. I remember when I was ten and playing football for Durham County, I would never drink at night so it wouldn't happen. But on the last night I had some cocoa and drinks ... and wet the bed.

CRAIG FARNAN: At Arbroath, Graham Buckley was told he was going to be on the bench for the cup game against Rangers and he was a bit depressed. Kenny MacDonald decided to make things worse by playing a joke on him at the hotel the night before the game. He cr****d on a piece of toilet paper and put it on Graham's chest as he lay sleeping and then everyone stood waiting until he woke up. Graham came to wondering what everyone was doing and didn't have a clue what was going on.

BRYN HALLIWELL (Clyde, St Johnstone, Hamilton): I was done over good and proper by the Wimbledon Crazy Gang on my eighteenth birthday. It was a really quiet start to the day and I thought I'd escaped any punishment. Then the rest of the keepers Neil Sullivan, Paul Heald and Kelvin Davies ganged up on me. They stripped me naked, handcuffed me to the goalposts for an hour and chucked manure at me. Training started and every time they lapped the park they kicked more manure at me. There were TV cameras, and photographers at the ground and worst of all a TV crew from America.

BARRY MCLAUGHLIN: I almost had my St Mirren career ended as a kid after a prank went wrong. I was an S-form at the time and during PE a few of us mooned at what we thought was the school netball team. It turned out to be group of eight-year-olds and the headmaster threatened to report us to St Mirren.

GLYNN HURST: I used to mess about with answerphone messages all the time when I was younger but I doubt if I could print any of the things I used to say and do. Perhaps the most printable thing I could tell you is I once left a message saying: "I'm on the nest right now, I'll give you a call back when I'm finished."

NIGEL QUASHIE: Going back to Portsmouth with Southampton, I was popular that day. They were calling me Judas and all the rest but then this ten-year-old at the side of the tunnel leaned over and roared: "Quashie, you stink of f***ing s**t!" He was so convincing and his face was so twisted that I had to have a little sniff to make sure I didn't.

JIM PATERSON: I was with my mates from Blantyre and one emptied another pal's bottle of Evian water and replaced it with some of the local tap water. He ended up with sickness and diarrhoea. He was still suffering four days later and he still doesn't know who did it.

DAVID ZDRILIC (Aberdeen): One time my old team-mate from Australia, Manis Lamond, was about to get a massage when he had a little accident. He was naked and bending over on to the table when he went to break wind and, well . . . followed through!

MARCO MAISANO (Morton): When I was thirteen, I was staying at a friend's house and ended up wetting the bed. When my pal's mum saw the big wet patch I just said I was hot and was sweating a lot but I think they could tell I was lying because it smelled.

ZANDER DIAMOND: I scored for Aberdeen against Rangers in a 1-1 draw with a certain part of my anatomy. The press asked me which part of my body it came off and I couldn't tell them so I just pointed. Next thing I know, I'm seeing headlines like "Cock of the North". That was embarrassing, especially for my family to read.

STEVE BOWEY: I have a mate called Preeny and one time when we were out, he went missing. Then all of a sudden he came running out of a cubicle completely naked with a trail of burning toiler paper coming out of his bottom. It set off the fire alarms and the bouncers tried to catch him but failed.

PETER MACDONALD: My favourite Gazza story is when he peed on Erik Bo Andersen at training. I was standing next to him at the time and it was hilarious. We were doing stretching exercises when Gazza whipped it out. Erik shouted how disgusting it was, the rest of us just thought, "That's Gazza for you!"

ALAN ROUGH: I swore on our radio show a few times. I said the word "sh**e" which I'm not allowed to say – it was along the lines of: "What a load of sh**e!" As soon as I said it I realised what I'd done, so I asked Ewen Cameron if I was allowed to say "sh**e" and then I said: "I won't say sh**e again then." Luckily I didn't get into trouble for it because they realised it was light-hearted.

ALEX WILLIAMS: Morton were staying at a hotel and John McCormack was giving us a team talk. He was wearing shorts that were a bit too loose. Put it this way, everything was hanging out. We couldn't concentrate on what he was saying.

MARTYN CORRIGAN: Years ago, I got nicked by the police when I was doing the toilet in an alley in Glasgow. When you have to go, you have to go. They let me go with a telling-off.

STEVEN THOMSON: My old Palace team-mate Gareth Davies would do things like take a dump in a player's shoe or something like that.

MARK MCGHEE: I was with Aberdeen and we were playing Porto away in the European Cup in front of 70,000 people. I got a shout from Gordon Strachan and when I turned round I couldn't believe my eyes – one of the Porto players was peeing in the middle of the pitch.

TREVOR MOLLOY: I have had Deep Heat in the underwear and it was after a game when we had been beaten. We were being held back in the dressing room and I was scratching away because my b***s were burning but all I could do was sit there. I got back at the guy who did it by taking his Armani suit and cutting it to ribbons.

SIMON MENSING: The St Johnstone players went on a night out and Kevin 'Dinky' Rutkiewicz and his mate Chris led me astray. We were downing shots and I made the mistake of thinking I could match them. I was bouncing off the walls when I came in while my girlfriend Janet had her friends round. I went through to the back garden and p**d on the shed. I slept on the couch and had a terrible hangover the next morning.

ROSS FORBES: Every time Jim O'Brien would go to the toilet, he'd tell us that's him going to drop the kids off at the pool. That was disgusting.

KEVIN RUTKIEWICZ: I spotted Ebbe Skovdahl going to the toilets at Pittodrie, so I decided to play a joke on him. I put on a long dark jacket, stuck on a pair of Teddy Scott's Eric Morecambe glasses and a balaclava. Ebbe was having a pee and I snuck up behind him. He turned round, got the fright of his life and almost fell into the urinal. I ran out of the toilet and back into the treatment room. But he knew it was me.

SCOTT CHAPLAIN: The boys were in the Shanghai Shuffle in Glasgow. We started quite early with the drinking and then some of the boys started peeing in the pond in the restaurant. Then someone put a chair in the pond and sat down to enjoy his drink. We got chucked out of every bar that night. We ended up in the Candy Bar and they wrote a letter to the club complaining that we flooded the toilets and chipped the paintwork. We had to explain it to Campbell Money but some of the claims were absolute nonsense. We were loud more than anything.

FRANK GRAY: John Robertson was quite a character at Nottingham Forest. He was a naturally funny guy and I remember he would go to the toilet for a sneaky cigarette and all you would see was the smoke coming out of the cubicle.

JIM MCALISTER: Dean Keenan is the only person I know who can do a No.2 on demand. I couldn't possibly tell you some of the places he has left a present.

ALEX KEDDIE: On a flight over to Malaga, we had a few drinks and when I went to stand up I forgot I had a drink on my table so it spilled all over me. I had this massive wet patch on my crotch and it looked as if I had peed myself. Everyone was laughing except for me.

ADAM COAKLEY: I went to Newcastle for my twenty-first for a weekend. We got a pink party bus all the way down. We kept stopping to pee on the hard shoulder.

DANNY GRAINGER: You could never go to the toilet in peace when Lee Wilkie was about. If you sat on the toilet, Lee would get a bucket of water and chuck it over the door.

X-Files

ARE footballers from another planet? Many seem to think so but some players genuinely believe in UFOs or ghosts. Others have just encountered surreal moments which they just can't explain . . .

NIGEL QUASHIE: Andy Impey at QPR was a lunatic. We were pre-season training in Richmond Park one day and he's s***-scared of horses. This woman is riding her nag and we're jogging along and Andy gets it into his head the horse is going to attack him. He makes for it and I thought he was going to chin this horse. Then he pulls the saddle off, the woman goes flying and he throws the saddle off the cliff. The woman was going ballistic. I've never seen anything like that.

JIM HAMILTON (Veteran striker of many SPL clubs): I'm called Flipper. Somehow a story surfaced that I had six toes and all of a sudden the Livingston fans starting calling me Flipper. I certainly don't have six toes and I have no idea why they thought

I did. Then the Motherwell fans started calling me it as well. Very strange.

COLIN STEWART: A group of us at Ross County were driving on the A9. Stan Taylor was driving when Charlie Adam suddenly grabbed the wheel. Stan tried to grab it back and we ended up on the other side of the road. We smashed through a bush, hit a couple of signs and landed perfectly in a parking bay. We just missed hitting a lorry and not long after a police car went by, but they didn't suspect anything was wrong. I still don't know why Charlie did it. He can be a bit spontaneous.

GERRY MCCABE: I once bumped into Bill Wyman at Central Station in Glasgow. The Stones had just finished a gig the same night Bayern Munich played Saint Etienne in the 1976 European Cup Final at Hampden. I asked him where Mick Jagger was. He said: "He takes the plane, I like taking the train!"

PAT STANTON: We were in Dublin for pre-season when John Brownlie said: "I've been here before." We asked if he meant Dublin but he said he had been here in another life. George Stewart asked who he was and John was quite serious when he said he was Davy Crockett. John Blackley asked him if he was at the Alamo, but John said he didn't remember much about it.

DYLAN KERR: I was in a bath naked except for my boots and having two headless chickens thrown in with me and getting covered in their blood. It was a ritual at Arcadia, the South African club I signed for. I also had to jump over fire and throw ash over the area of the pitch I played on. I remember playing a game once and afterwards the opposition's witch doctor got lynched in Durban because we came back from two goals down to win 3–2. We were still in the dressing room at the time.

CRAIG MCKEOWN: I woke up fully clothed lying next to naked Stevie Masterton after Michael McGowan's engagement party. There was an arm and a leg over me and he woke up and looked up at me and said, "Hold me!"

COLIN MURDOCK (Hibs): At Manchester United I was sharing digs with Keith Gillespie when I saw a ghost at the end of my bed. I actually thought it was Keith because he is quite pale and ghost-like, so I told him to get back to bed. But when I turned round Keith was already in his bed. I hid under my covers for the rest of the night. When I mentioned it to the landlady she said she had seen it before. I've also seen a UFO but I don't want to go into that.

RAY STEWART (Dundee United, West Ham, Scotland): The strangest training session we had was when John Lyall made us go through an assault course at West Ham. It felt like SAS training when we were crawling about on the ground in combat gear. It was daft but the reason he did it was to toughen us up. We even tossed cabers!

JIMMY BONE (Partick Thistle, St Mirren, Hearts): Before a cup final game in Africa, the opposition cut a chicken's neck and the players walked over the blood. That was a bit intimidating for my players but I just told them that Scottish magic is better than that.

JOHN MCVEIGH: I took Robert Duvall down to Strathclyde Park and was trying to teach him how to kick the ball. These four young boys came over and recognised him and shouted: "Bobby! Ye want a drink?" and they offered him a drink of their bottle of Buckfast. I couldn't believe it.

STEVE PATERSON: I was with Manchester United on a tour of America in 1978 when we were about to play a Texan team in fancy dress. We went in cowboy outfits and they dressed up as Red Indians. We came out the tunnel and went round the pitch in stagecoaches with fake guns pretending to shoot each other. It was funny to see players like Joe Jordan, Lou Macari, Sammy McIlroy and Jimmy Nicholl doing that.

LEE WILKIE: I was in Bosnia with the Scotland Under-21s. That was unbelievable. On the bus from the airport you could see that every single house was riddled with bullet holes. The towns and villages were in ruins from the war. It was awful seeing all the graves as well. On the way to the game there were people in the streets cooking dogs. Our hotel was scary because it was bright yellow and it hadn't been touched. When you looked out the window to the hotel across the road it had a huge hole in it and bullet holes.

ANDY MCLAREN: When I first went to the AA meetings one woman came up to me and started chatting to me saying she knew who I was. It wasn't until five minutes into the conversation I realised she thought I was Gary Lineker. I didn't have the heart to tell her the truth and she is probably telling people she went to AA meetings with Gary Lineker.

LEE MAKEL: I was in Mexico on a jungle tour in speed boats but ours broke down and we were left behind. It was raining heavily. It was so quiet then all of a sudden I saw these eyes pop out of the water and it was a crocodile watching us. I just turned white. Luckily the leader of the tour came back and we were safe.

MARK DOBIE: Something strange happened while I was driving on a quiet country road in the Lake District after a game. It was two in the morning when something came alongside my car with three huge lights which were red, blue and green. It seemed to be feet away and then it disappeared into the distance. The most bizarre thing was there was no noise from it. I haven't a clue to this day what it was. People laugh at folk who say they have experienced things, but I am not one to tell lies.

CHRIS HILLCOAT: Big Ian Macfarlane fell ill one night on holiday in Spain and we went up the road early. The same thing happened the next night and we couldn't work out what was wrong with him. I came home a lot later and when I walked into the room he sat bolt upright on his bed and said, "Your sister is in the cupboard!" He then slumped back on the bed. I just s**t myself. I was even daft enough to look in the cupboard! He was ill the next day still so we got the doctor in. He said he had chicken pox and because he was drinking, he had hallucinated. He spent the rest of the week in the hotel room.

DAVID WINNIE: I was in the passenger seat in a car with Brian Hamilton driving on the motorway in Australia when all of a sudden this huge hairy spider appeared on the dashboard. Right away Brian pulled the handbrake up and of course the spider landed on my lap. There are a few poisonous ones and some that are harmless – luckily, it turned out to be harmless but I didn't know that. I jumped out the car in the middle of the motorway and started battering the spider. That was scary.

HARRY CAIRNEY: When I was just a boy, I used to get up in the middle of the night to go to the toilet and would see a little girl with blonde hair. Eventually I would be too scared to get up to go. The weird thing was, I looked at my daughter Sarah and realised she looked the spitting image of the girl I used to see at night. I do not think the girl I saw was a ghost but I don't know if I imagined it or if it was a reflection.

DAVE MACKINNON (Partick, Airdrie, Rangers, Kilmarnock): I was with Rangers when we went on a tour of Iraq in December. We stayed in Baghdad during their war with Iran and at eleven o'clock at night you would hear the air raid sirens going off. We met Saddam Hussein and he told us the Iranians were the aggressors and Iraqis were peace loving. Then he gave us a gold pen to take home.

KENNY CLARK: I refereed a Champions League qualifier in Luxembourg between Avenir Beggen and Galatasaray, with John Underhill and Stuart Dougal the linesmen. The segregation wasn't good so it was chaotic and John got laid out by a bag of pistachios that skelped him on the head.

DAVIE NICHOLLS: We used to get chased by dogs at Clydebank's training ground. There was this one Alsatian dog which always came on the park in the middle of our five-a-side games and one day it got a bit of a shock when Gordon Chisholm volleyed the ball straight at it. The irate owner, an old woman, started swearing at us and asked who had hurt her dog. No one was brave enough to own up. It was a junkie's playground and there were needles and bottles on the ground. Sometimes we couldn't even train properly because the council had trucks on the pitch – it was total madness.

TAM MCMANUS: I've played alongside an unidentified object – Paul Lovering. He has to be some sort of alien. He won't win any beauty contests. To be fair Paul, neither will I.

CHRISTIAN DAILLY (Dundee United, Rangers, Scotland): Rod Stewart felt like rewarding me for getting him tickets to the Latvia match a few years back when we qualified for the World Cup. He called me on my mobile. I turned to my mates and said: "It's Rod Stewart!" He asked me to go to London for a party but I had to tell him: "Sorry Rod, not tonight – I'm going to Dundee."

TAM MACDONALD: One night I dreamed that I had been abducted by aliens and they swept me away in a big scary craft to a strange land full of strange people. When I woke up I was in Cumnock!

DANNY INVINCIBILE: When I was about eight, Ian Botham lived in the house next to mine in Australia. He's really scared of spiders and he once asked my brother Dominic to catch one that was in his attic. You can't forget a name like Invincibile and it would be interesting to ask him about the hell that we put him through as neighbours. He gave my brother a signed cricket ball though.

JIM STEWART: When I was a youngster at Kilmarnock, I played with Tommy McLean and he and a couple of other guys swiped the car keys of a player called David Swan. They rolled his Mini through the old foyer doors at Rugby Park and left it in the reception area. Davie came out into the car park and couldn't find his car anywhere. He wasn't too happy and neither was the manager when he saw the car in the middle of reception. I've never seen anything like it in my life.

KEVIN KYLE: I stayed in a hostel with half a dozen other players when I was a youth player at Sunderland. The house next door had been knocked down after a kid was murdered in it. It happened years ago but it used to spook us a little bit. One night I placed a jam jar on the middle of the work-top. All of a sudden it slid off the table and smashed on the floor. We were scared stiff.

We'd also regularly hear the toilet flush during the night when no one was using it.

RICKY GILLIES: This will sound crazy, but I've had quite a few out-of-body experiences. It's hard to explain, but I can be lying on the couch, watching TV, and feel myself falling asleep. If someone was to come and stand beside me, I would be aware that they were there and would be able to hear them, but wouldn't be able to move. I can actually see them in my mind's eye but have to make the effort to push my body and wake myself up. As I say, it's bizarre but completely true.

IAN HARTY (Stranraer, Clyde): When I go to the Showcase Cinema in Coatbridge I am scared to go in the toilets. I don't know what it is but every time I go in, there is no one there and it's very quiet. It gives me the creeps.

ALLAN PRESTON: I went to Costa Rica to watch potential signings. When I met the agent, he was carrying a knife and a gun! He told me he had to have them in case someone tried to rob us, as the area we were in near the border with Nicaragua was dangerous. Apparently, robbers bump your car and when you get out, they shoot you. When I went to a game there I was the only white guy in the 10,000 crowd. I got a lot of bad looks and they were shouting at me to leave.

WILLIE MILLER: After we lost 4-1 to Brazil at the '82 World Cup, I was selected, along with Socrates, for a drugs test. The heat was searing and it took me a while to get enough fluids in me to pass water. I requested some diet Coke while Socrates asked for two beers and twenty cigarettes. Here was this great Brazilian sipping a bottle of beer and puffing away telling me how he was a qualified doctor.

NEIL BARRETT: I was on a Christmas night out in Bournemouth with the Portsmouth lads. I was dressed up as Dino from *The Flintstones* but it was the sight of 6ft 7in Peter Crouch dressed up as a shark and getting refused entry to a club because he was pretty drunk which was a bit surreal. He actually tried to bite the bouncer with his costume.

ALEX WILLIAMS: I was on my way to training at Stirling Albion when I was attacked by a flock of seagulls. I was walking through an industrial estate when there were hundreds of them trying to get at me. I had to run away.

GARY DEMPSEY: The strangest experience I've ever had was a lost two-and-a-half hours with Noel Hunt. We flew over to Dublin and by the time we got to Wexford it was about 1am. We only had one-and-a-half hours drinking time left so we were downing shots like crazy. We were getting stupidly drunk and left the place at 2.30am. But after that, I just can't remember what happened and neither can Noel. For, what should have been a ten-minute journey back to mine took us two-and-a-half hours because we arrived at 5am. To this day we don't know what happened in between.

FRANK MCGARVEY: I was with St Mirren in 1976 when we went to the Caribbean. When we arrived for a game in Surinam, they turned the floodlights on and there were about 2,000 frogs all over the pitch. The bus driver got a brush and started sweeping them off.

JOHN BURRIDGE: I've actually seen a space ship. It was Christmas day when I was playing for Newcastle around 1987 or '88. I was driving home and there was no one on the road when I saw this big light over the mountains. I was quite frightened. My wife Janet rang the police and it emerged that several people had spotted a UFO in that area.

DAVID PROCTOR: I had to share a tiny single room with Darren Thomson at Caley, and the beds were basically right next to each other. It was like a scene out of *Planes, Trains and Automobiles*. Darren had a line of his clothes down the middle to separate our space and he would moan if I had anything on his side of the room.

DAVE BAIKIE: I've been electrocuted while I was working and I was thrown ten feet back. Both my hands were burnt. Another time, I was working on a building site when I wanted to make myself a cup of tea. I lit the gas oven to heat it up but it blew up in my face and my eyelids were stuck together because my eye lashes had been singed and were welded firmly together.

STEWART HILLIS: The strangest thing I ever did was sit on a dark road near the runway in Portugal with Ally McCoist, who had just broken his leg, and an administrator. We by-passed the airport checks and were sitting waiting in the middle of nowhere. I had a cheeky wee bottle of red wine and decided to open it up, so we just sat there drinking until we were taken to the plane.

MIKE FRASER: I kept getting strange deliveries outside my door. It happened about ten times. I had bags of clothes, tinned food, cans of beer, cuppa soup, shooting and fishing magazines, a haggis and forty DVDs. I have no idea whether it was a prank or not. The DVDs weren't even any good as they are all Jean-Claude Van Damme films. I'm running out of space to keep it all.

GARY MCSWEGAN: When Dundee United played Trabzonspor, there was a mosque with lots of wailing coming from it behind Sieb Dykstra's goal. Sieb went up to the referee to complain about it. He tried to get them to stop it because it was putting him off.

JIM BALLANTYNE: Every time we are in the Brechin City boardroom it's a strange experience. The hospitality there knows no bounds. There is a picture in their boardroom of Gillian doing the splits on the boardroom table. Obviously it was down to the drink as they kept topping up our glasses.

GORDON SMITH: I met Paul McCartney three times. I was at a Wings concert in Glasgow when the head of security, who wanted my autograph, said he could introduce me to Paul and Linda. Paul said he was a big football fan and said he would love to see me play when I was transferred to Brighton. Then I was invited to one of Linda's photo exhibitions and I couldn't believe he remembered who I was. He even invited me to his house in Sussex. I mentioned I played guitar and would play the song 'Blackbird'. He got his guitar and played 'Blackbird' in front of me. Luckily he has a left-handed guitar so couldn't ask me to play it. It will live with me for the rest of my life.

JIM LAUCHLAN: During Charlie Miller's stag do in Las Vegas we went for a helicopter ride over the Grand Canyon, but Barry Ferguson and I had stayed out late and we were bladdered. I went on the tour, but fell asleep and never saw the Grand Canyon at all.

You Don't Say

HERE is where we delve a little into the subject matter ... what makes them tick? What are they scared of? Tell us something we don't know about you ...

TONY BULLOCK: I am a member of the Erasure fan club and I once saw them play eight times in twenty-eight days. I travelled the country to see them in Manchester, Milton Keynes, Whitley Bay and London. My wife thinks I have slight gay tendencies. I like cheesy '80s music and I am always on the dancefloor with my cheesy dancing.

STEVE PATERSON: I like black cats running out in front of my car for good luck. I bought a black cat called Diesel so when I came home it could cross my path but it just slept all day. I also ran over a black cat a few years ago – maybe it isn't lucky!

JOHN HUGHES: I've had armed police storm my house thinking I was a bank robber. I was driving back from Falkirk with a group of players when we spotted a lot of police cars at a bank with their sirens on and I slowed down to get a look. At teatime, the police were banging on the door. Somebody had taken down my number and said we looked suspicious. Eventually they realised and were full of apologies.

CHRIS BURKE (Rangers, Cardiff): I really don't like cats. In fact, I hate them. They're evil. There is a group of them that come up the stairs to the landing of my flat and they terrify me. I opened my door one time and they were there. I poured water over them and they ran away.

PAUL LAWSON: The guys at Ross County call me J-Lo because the size of my a**e. I have been slagged off about it since I started out at Celtic.

JACKIE MCNAMARA SENIOR (Hibs, Celtic): I was once branded a Communist in a newspaper. On the same page was a story about ice skater John Curry being a homosexual. The stories ran side by side in the paper and my dad told me at least they didn't get the pictures mixed up and accused John of being a Communist and me of being a homosexual!

JOSE QUITONGO (Hearts, Hamilton and Angolan nutter): The only thing I did before a game was touch the ground and bless myself. I'm not even religious. I once saw the Brazil players do it and I thought, "If it works for them, it works for me."

STEPHEN SIMMONS: Craig Gordon won't be happy at me mentioning it because he probably hasn't been called this in a long time but he used to be called 'Shania' after the singer Shania Twain because he walks like a woman. Maybe they will start calling him it again.

DAVIE IRONS: I met Michael Jackson at Disney World in Florida and have the pictures to prove it. We went into a small gift shop when he came up to me and said Lewis was a beautiful baby and could he take a picture. When I heard him speak it dawned on me it was Jacko even though he was wearing shades, a hat and a Chinese moustache. He was with Lisa-Marie Presley and it was just after all the child abuse allegations came out.

SCOTT STRUTHERS: I'm actually a qualified Glasgow Underground train driver. I bid £75 in a Cash For Kids auction for a day's course. I have a certificate to prove it. I can also talk to you in Klingon – because I am a Star Trek fanatic. Also, I'm nowhere near as old as I look. Unbelievable.

MARCO RUITENBEEK: I have no problems at all buying lingerie for my wife. I don't feel embarrassed about it and she also buys me underwear. I am a very good judge when it comes to buying women's undies.

JIMMY BONE: I feared for my life in an African Cup game quarter-final in Burkino Faso. We were winning 1-0 but then suddenly the lights went out – and I was the only white man in a crowd of 32,000 people. They were trying to get the game called off. There were riot police around me so it was quite scary because you don't know what might happen. We even had to run the gauntlet back to the hotel.

JOHN MCVEIGH: Sandy Stewart is the most boring person I know. We call him Ted Striker after the character in *Airplane* where he bores everyone to death.

JOHN HUGHES: A lot of people say I look a lot like Arnold Schwarzenegger. I have a mate called Cheb and he is about 5ft 4ins and is the double of Danny de Vito – you should see us out together. We look like we are from that film *Twins*. We get a lot of stick.

STEWART EASTON: On holiday in Crete, we took a boat trip and when we anchored I jumped in the sea for a swim. Next thing, I felt like I was tangled up in seaweed, but when I looked down there was an octopus on my leg. It was only a baby one, but they're still scary. I shook it off but it came back at me and by the time I got free my leg was covered in little round sucker marks. I showed the captain where it was – he hooked it out of the water, killed it and took it home for his dinner.

WILLIE BENNETT (Whitehill Welfare): I started playing the trombone at school and was even asked to play in the school band but I wisely chose football instead because I lived in Muirhouse in Edinburgh and couldn't be seen walking with a trombone case because I'd get beaten up. If you are carrying a case there then you're usually carrying drugs or a machine gun.

CRAIG HINCHCLIFFE: I once appeared on *The Big Breakfast*. I was sitting watching it one day when they had a feature called 'Snogger from Heaven'. A girl came on and said she wanted to find a guy she snogged in Magaluf and she had a picture of him. I was sitting there watching it thinking I had been to Magaluf when Gaby Roslin flashed a picture of me. My dad was also watching and he spat out his tea and toast. The following week they paid for me to come down and appear on the show.

CAMPBELL MONEY: The weirdest superstition I have witnessed was one of John Burridge's. He would always go out and do cartwheels before a game.

BARRY ROBSON: I played Oor Wullie in a school play when I was in primary seven at Strathburn Primary School in Inverurie. I ran on stage with a bucket, my dungarees and spikey hair in front of the whole school. I have never acted since then.

GED BRANNAN: I have a birthmark on my bum.

DAVIE NICHOLLS: I'm great at chess. I used to go to classes after school and for a while I even kept a diary of all my favourite moves to do them again. I once played a grandmaster at Bellshill and drew with him, and when I was at Hibs, I tricked Gordon

Hunter by saying I'd beat him in five moves. He didn't have a clue how good I was and I shocked him.

TAM MCMANUS: When I was warming up in an Edinburgh derby for Hibs, a Hearts fan near their dug-out stuck her tongue out at me. She was a bit of a looker so I stuck my tongue out back at her. A few days later, I got a letter from her addressed "to the Hibee with the cheeky smile". I decided to get in touch with her. We met up and got on really well. Mind you, I know I'll get pelters from the fans for dating a Hearts supporter.

ALAN COMBE: I am incredibly superstitious. You name a superstition and I've got it. I'll make new ones up every day to try and bring more luck to my game. Sometimes I take a fancy for Red Bull before a game. I did it once, played a blinder and vowed to do it every week. I also buy a new pair of socks for every game. I try to eat the same things too, although one week I ate a bowl of macaroni cheese before the Killie game and ended up in the toilet for most of the day. I vowed never to do it again but then saw I got a 9 in the *SunSport* ratings and changed my mind again.

BRIAN MCPHEE: I am ashamed to admit this but when I was nine I used to collect car registration numbers. I did this for about six months until one of my pals pointing out that it was a decidedly freaky thing to do.

CHRIS MCGROARTY: I used to be scared of the Mr T poster in my room. It's a bit embarrassing because I had a wee brother who was four at the time and I was six and it bothered me more than him. I'd wake up in the night and scare myself into thinking he was really there.

CRAIG DARGO: Kevin Twaddle and Keith Wright would both bore me talking about their goals all the time. Keith would always goes on about his goal in the League Cup final for Hibs and Kevin has told me the story about his hat-trick at Stranraer so many times I can mime it behind his back. I'm fed up hearing about how a fan ran on the pitch, gave him a high five and was lifted by a steward after No.3.

STEVEN BOYACK: At Rangers they used to call me 'Schumacher' because of my likeness to the Formula One driver Michael. But at Dundee my name was ten times worse, all because Scott Wilson thought he would have a laugh just before I left Ibrox. He started calling me 'Tweetie Pie' because he said I looked like the cartoon character – and then the gaffer started calling me it.

BILLY MCNEILL: Believe it or not I think I have Obsessive Compulsive Disorder, but only when it comes to dishwashers. I won't allow anyone else in the house to fill it and when they do I empty it and put it back in using the correct 'McNeill System'.

NIGEL QUASHIE: My nickname was 'Quashie-Modo'. I got that one at Nottingham Forest. They have this thing there that you pull a name out of a hat and you have to buy that player a Christmas present. Andy Johnson got me a bell and a *Hunchback of Notre Dame* video. I've still got that bell in my garage. The best nickname I ever heard was for a Norwegian player at Forest called Jon Helder. He was called 'Knock Knock' because when you spoke to him it was as if the lights were on and nobody was home.

DEREK MCINNES: Ally McCoist had his license taken off him for drink-driving and I lived closest to him. No, that's not true actually – Gazza lived closer but he couldn't be trusted to look after himself. I'd spend half the morning sitting in his driveway waiting on him to go to training. Coisty tells the story that I only got an extension to my contract at Rangers because he needed me to drive him around.

WILLIE FALCONER: Elton John let me drive his Bentley when I was at Watford. He was the chairman at the time and one day all the players were outside, admiring the motor. Elton came outside and I told him I thought it was a beautiful car. He threw me the keys and let me take it for a spin. I only drove it around the car park at Vicarage Road, and the truth is his chauffeur sat in the passenger seat to make sure I didn't run away with it. It was still fantastic.

ALLAN PRESTON: There must be some kind of valve on my backside because it keeps getting bigger.

DARREN YOUNG: When I was a lot younger, I went out one Saturday even though we had a heavy training session on the Sunday. I had my first real hangover – pounding head, sore stomach . . . the works. I covered by claiming I had eaten a dodgy microwave meal. I ended up being let off training and went for a sleep in the treatment room while they had training. Roy Aitken was the manager at the time so it is just as well I wasn't caught.

RUSSELL DUNCAN: After we beat Celtic 1-0 in the Scottish Cup at Inverness, Stevie Hislop was giving Graeme Stewart a piggy back but Bryan Gilfillan pushed them and Stevie split his chin and dislocated his finger when he fell over. He came into training the next day with a stookie on his finger and stitches on his chin. Donald Park was raging at him.

ALEX WILLIAMS: Chris Millar really loves himself. He was in some magazine looking for women to date him while he was at Morton. I also shared a room with Jim Thomson at Queen of the South and he borrowed my Hugo Boss jacket once. He tried to pass it off as his. Someone asked if it was a new jacket and he said something like: "Nothing but the best for me."

DARREN MACKIE: We found out Ryan Esson had been taking dancing lessons. We found out his fiancée had been getting him lessons for their upcoming wedding. He kept this hidden from the boys for about three months but somehow it leaked out and he got absolute pelters for it.

BRIAN IRVINE (Aberdeen, Dundee, Ross County): Bobby Connor has been known as Roger since he was called Roger Connor in a match report. Even his wife calls him Roger.

BRYAN GILFILLAN: I have the hairiest legs known to man but you can't really see them because they are blond. I sometimes think about shaving them. I don't think the boys would let me get away with it. The physio goes on about how much oil he has to rub in.

FRANK MCGARVEY: We were in Singapore with St Mirren in 1987 when Tommy Wilson and I ate a rare one-hundred-year-old egg at a function. We were playing in a tournament and I was so ill after eating it. I told Alex Smith I had to come off the pitch but he had used up all his subs and then the game went into extra time. When I came back home I was in bed for two days. I was so ill I don't even know if we won the tournament.

18

You're a Very Naughty Boy

ARE footballers invincible? Do they get away with murder? Judge for yourself as they tell us the worst things they have ever done.

TONY BULLOCK: I was out with the lads at Ross County after a game against Raith Rovers. I ended up pulling my trousers down and mooning but I got caught on CCTV. I was arrested, spent a night in the cells and got fined £450. My wife wasn't very happy.

TOM STEVEN: I was in Perth, Australia, with former Rangers and Hearts player George Donaldson. We were stopped by the police and asked our names and details. I said that we were footballers and I think they thought we were joking. They then asked me to get in the back of the car, but I ended up bolting it as I heard stories about people getting beaten up in the back of police cars. I got a good 150 yards away when I heard him say, "Halt, police!" He fired his gun in the air and my legs went. I ended up crawling commando-style into some bushes and got home. They came to my door, but my sister said I wasn't in. For about a month I was on the toilet every time the doorbell rang.

GERRY COLLINS: I went on holiday with my two pals to Torquay. They told me they were going to check on the hotel and told me to stay in the car. They didn't come back after an hour so I went to find them and saw them in the back of a police car. I told the cops they had my two pals and they handcuffed me and put me in the car. It turns out my pals tried to steal the money from a phone box. I never knew what they were doing and I got let out.

ALEX WILLIAMS: I met a girl in a nightclub and we exchanged phone numbers. We arranged to meet up and I hopped in a taxi. But I couldn't remember what she looked like. When I did spot her I just told the taxi driver to keep going and switched my phone off. When I eventually turned it back on she was straight on, calling me an a******e!

COLIN MILLER (Hamilton): I once went to lunch with the Queen and Duke of Edinburgh and nicked the cutlery. It was a lunch to honour the Athlete of the Year for British Columbia and I was one of the nominees because I was the youngest player in the North American Soccer League at the time and came from Vancouver. I didn't win, but it was still a tremendous thrill and I stole the cutlery from the hotel as a souvenir. My folks still have it at home.

IAN DURRANT: Ally McCoist and I got caught up in a street fight in East Kilbride and were taken in for questioning. We sat there having a nightmare when this stern sergeant came in and barked: "Right Mr McCoist, do you have a police record?" The bold boy answers: "Yes . . . 'Walking on the Moon.'" Bad situation, but a great one-liner.

ALEX TOTTEN: Walter Smith and I had a bust-up in the tunnel when Rangers were at McDiarmid Park. Ally McCoist elbowed John Inglis and I was shouting to Wattie in the dug-out and he was shouting back at me. One thing led to another and we had a bad argument in the tunnel at half time. Next thing the police lifted us. The police commander asked us to leave the ground. Wattie and I ended up going to a director David Sidie's house and his wife got a terrible fright when we turned up at quarter past four. We missed the whole second half and went back to the ground at six o'clock. We ended up in court. Wattie and I were passing Polo Mints to each other in the dock.

JOHN HILLCOAT: At Dumbarton, there were a group of us in a car, including Craig Brittain and Andy Brown, who were stopped by police. None of us were wearing seat belts but they singled me out even though I was in the back seat. But then one of them recognised Andy and we managed to bribe them with tickets for a Dumbarton game in return for not booking me.

KEVIN KYLE: Some girl sold a story about me to the *Sunday Sport*. She said I was great in bed and was very well-endowed. The headline was all about how I was the best in the Premiership. The paper phoned Peter Reid before they ran the story and he told me it would be in. On the Sunday morning I got up at the crack of dawn and ran down to the local paper shop and bought a copy. I couldn't believe it. They even had an eleven-inch ruler beside my picture.

BRIAN MCGINTY: I was in a French class at school when my pal Callum MacGregor was struggling with his vocabulary. He was told if he didn't get the next one right he would have to stand for the rest of class. He was asked the French for cheese and you could see he didn't know. He looked at me for help and I told him – while trying not to laugh – "le cheddar". He repeated what I said and the whole class just fell about laughing.

RONNIE MACDONALD: When I was at Knightswood, I played with a guy called John MacKintosh who used to be the main bouncer at the Savoy disco in Glasgow. I was in goal against Hamilton FP and one of their strikers left the boot in. John did his bit to protect me by knocking out THREE of their players, getting lifted by the police and getting the match abandoned. He was banned from the game for a year.

COLIN MILNE: My best man Tony and I were messing about having a dummy fight in the street opposite a nightclub. We were rolling about on the deck when the police came along, thought we were serious, and lifted us. They put us in jail. My uncle works in the CID and when he spotted my best mate at the desk he asked:

"What are YOU doing here?" Tony replied: "Me? Martin's already in the slammer!" He looked around and gave me pelters.

GAVIN RAE: I remember being in the Dundee youth team when Jim Hamilton and Paul Tosh wrecked my flat. They stole the keys from my pocket during training, stuck dead fish in my bed, sprayed shaving foam all over the bed, turned the dining table upside down and threw clothes everywhere. I got home and laughed, I knew they had done it.

CRAIG TAGGART: I would dog school and write fake notes saying, "Please excuse Craig from school today because he wisnae well and couldnae be bothered." Needless to say, the next day my mum was waiting for me at the school gates.

CHRISTIAN DAILLY: David Bowman was horrible to me at Dundee United and he also enjoyed winding up the office girls. In the days before computers, they used to spend hours counting out thousands of match tickets. Davie would be in the place two minutes and he'd wreck the piles and scatter them all over the floor.

STEVIE TOSH: I once set fire to the Raith commercial manager's hair! We went on a '70s theme night at Christmas and we all had wigs on. Dave Bowman thought it would be funny to set about them with a lighter. We pestered a few people and they all found it funny. Then a few hours, and loads more drink later, I saw a woman who I thought had a wig on. I set the lighter but it caught some hairspray and went alight. I had to desperately put it out and apologise unreservedly. It was a silly prank and I'd like to say: "Kids don't try that at home please."

PAUL MARTIN (Dumbarton, Albion Rovers): I had a fight with Martin Melvin after a game at Dumbarton. He headbutted me and bust my nose and I punched him and knocked his two front teeth out. I needed four stitches on my hand after it and nobody could stop us. We soon made up and forgot about it and I think it was the best thing that could happen. As far as I'm concerned you need fights and tension on the training ground because it means you have a team full of winners.

SCOTT WALKER: I sold one of my old workmates a dodgy Ford Fiesta. I told him it drove like a dream and was a snip at £600. In reality, nearly everything needed fixing and it was worth a packet of sweets and no more. I saw him a few months later and when I asked him how the car was going he claimed "like a dream".

NIGEL PEPPER: When I was a wild teenager at Rotherham, one of my team-mates got his hands on a whole load of knocked off car radios and had to flog them quickly because they were so hot. I helped him out by flogging a few of them to people I knew in pubs and places like that. The police got onto the case and my mate claimed he knew nothing about them being knocked off and gave a false description to the cops. That threw them right off course and we got off with it.

KENNY BLACK (Hearts, Airdrie): When I was at Portsmouth, a few of us went to Salisbury racecourse and were struggling to get tickets to get in. Then I saw an envelope at the gate with the name Mark Usher on it. They guy at the gate handed over the tickets when I said I was Mark Usher and we had a great night. So if he's reading this – sorry Mark.

OWEN ARCHDEACON (Celtic): As a teenager going to training at Celtic Boys Club, I used to dodge paying the train fare. I used to try and hide behind the seat hoping the conductor wouldn't see me and I could save the money for a bag of chips after training. I only did it when I felt hungry.

BILLY MCNEILL: Jimmy Johnstone bought a car from our masseur Jimmy Steel who had the registration plate V14. Steely's mistake was not to take his private plates off the car because he assumed Jinky would do it and restore it to the original plate. The wee man was driving around with V14 clocking up speeding fines and getting up to his usual mischief. The cops nicked Steely and told him "You can't go driving around with Jinky's plates on your car, sir!"

ERIK PAARTALU: Colin Stewart and Alex Walker are always up to something at Morton. One day, they decided to get everyone's keys and steal our cars and move them. One of the young lads Troy had his car taken all the way to Bridge of Weir and he spent the afternoon with our goalie coach Davie Wylie trying to find it.

ALLAN RUSSELL: I was at Hibs as a kid when Tam McManus and another player called Jaffa decided to nick this battered old Metro belonging to a boy called Graeme Bryson. They said they were just going to move it but when he found the car it was a mess. They had lost control, veered into oncoming traffic then hit a wall. It was a write-off.

STEVEN MCGARRY: I got in trouble with Ryan Robinson a few years ago. We were on our way back from Blackpool, where we'd played a pre-season game, and stopped off at a joke shop. Everyone bought something and we were all having a laugh on the way back up the road. I bought a pop gun. A few days later, Giggsy asked me to give him a lift home from training and the gun was lying in the back seat of the car. While we were driving through Paisley, he rolled the window down, leaned out and pretended to shoot at people. It was just a laugh – although the gun made a noise it wasn't anything like a real gun – but people must have taken down my registration number and phoned the police because later that night I answered the door to two coppers. They genuinely thought we were shooting at people and insisted on searching my car, even after I had given them the toy gun. The fiscal got involved but we just had our wrists slapped.

TAM MCMANUS: When I was on the Hibs' ground staff, we had to pack away hundreds of selection boxes for local schools. It was a few days to pay day and Alan Russell and Martin Hughes and I were all skint. We took a few boxes each – there were so many we thought they wouldn't be missed – but we were wrong.

There was a knock on the door and in came youth coach Donald Park. We were all fined and given a clip around the ear.

SCOTT MCLEAN: Martin Hardie and I were on a moped in Ayia Napa and ended up getting chased by the police because we weren't wearing helmets. Martin jumped off the moped and ran away while I followed behind him on the bike. We must have hid for about five hours before going back out.

STEVE BOWEY: I spent twenty-four days in jail while I was in the army for going AWOL. I was confined to my bed for seven days with food poisoning until the Friday but I felt better and went home like the rest of the lads on the Thursday. When I got back on Sunday they said I should have been in bed so they put me away. The military police would make me do all kinds of things. One made me do press-ups and name the whole Manchester United squad, including reserves, before I could go to the toilet.

RICHIE FORAN: I've been convicted twice. I was up for assault for fighting in a Carlisle nightclub. A guy threw a pint over me for no reason so I had a scuffle with him. I pleaded guilty and got 150 hours community service. The second time was a farce in a game against Lincoln. I was sent off after eight minutes and we were down to eight men while they had ten. They missed a penalty and me, the chairman and some players cheered from the stand. We were told to leave the stand and then there was a big scuffle in the tunnel where we tried to watch the end of the game. The chairman and I both got charged with affray and we pleaded not guilty but we were both found guilty. I got 200 hours community service and a £900 fine.

MICHAEL MOORE: When I was at St Johnstone, a supporter wrote in and complained that I had been in a strip joint in Glasgow. They said I shouldn't be out and should have been concentrating on my football. Jim Weir got hold of the letter and read it out in front of everyone in the dressing room. Aggie the tea lady didn't speak to me for a couple of weeks and called me a pervert. There were other players there too, but I never grassed them up.

FRAZER WRIGHT: I haven't been in trouble with the police but that's because they never caught me. I was out with my mates in Glasgow when we stuck some traffic cones on our heads. The police chased us and they caught one of my mates David and he spent the night in the cells.

CRAIG MCEWAN: I once told a driver I had to go into my house to get some money and got him to drop me off a few streets from my house. He wouldn't let me go unless I gave him something so I gave him my jumper. I got out, jumped lots of fences and ran through a back garden while some folk were having a barbecue at 4am. I got home and could see the driver raging as he drove past looking for me.

COLIN CRAMB: Back at Bristol, I got involved in a fight on a night out. We had lost the derby 2-1 and I was standing at the bar having a drink with my girlfriend. Five guys were standing behind me and one kept flicking bits of paper at me. After the third time, I clocked the guy and stuck the head on him and tried to bite his nose. His other four friends waded in and leathered me and I ended up with thirty stitches.

CRAIG SAMSON: Mark Roberts was at Gus MacPherson's testimonial dinner but was seated at the back of the room so he wouldn't cause any bother. It didn't work as Mark ended up setting the tablecloth on fire.

RYAN MCCANN: Within two weeks of me joining Clyde, I ended up in the cells overnight after I tried to stop a fight between two of our players. The ironic thing was it was a night out for me to get to know the lads.

DAVID ROWSON: At Aberdeen, Kevin Christie was having his driving test and some of the boys – Hugh Robertson and Kenny Gilbert – decided to jump in their cars and follow him and the instructor. They did everything to put him off and succeeded – he failed his test.

BOBBY RUSSELL (Rangers, Motherwell): Dave McPherson was playing for Hearts and he told us Allan Moore had been stopped for speeding. My wife phoned up pretending to be a policewoman and told him to report to the station at 5pm the next day. She said if he didn't report he would receive a caution and a massive fine. But the following night Hearts had a big European game and he was pleading and saying he couldn't come. We eventually told him it was a joke and he wasn't happy.

JIM MCALISTER: I was driving the Morton boys through Paisley town centre when Dean Keanan leaned out the window and shouted abuse at people. Unknown to us there was an under-cover police car ahead of us which stopped us and told us off. I had to go into the station to hand in all my details as I was driving.

19

Yuck!

YOU probably don't want to be eating during this chapter. It is self-explanatory! Hope you have a strong stomach for their depraved antics.

MATT GLENNON: At Bolton, guys like John McGinlay would take the cakes you find at the bottom of urinals and put them among the biscuits in the lounge after games. You would get people biting into them thinking they were real cakes. Luckily I was never caught out.

COLIN CRAMB: Frankie Ness was the physio at Hamilton Accies and he told me about the time he stuck Pedigree Chum in his wife's sandwiches. She'd ask what he'd made her for her lunch and he would tell her it was potted meat.

PAUL SHEERIN: I was on the bench for Southampton – my one and only time – for a match against Blackburn at the Dell. Dave Merrington was the manager and was going mental at a decision when his false teeth came flying out his mouth. He brushed the dirt off and put them back in, pretending nothing happened.

DANNY CADAMARTERI: One of my team-mates had an upset stomach and tried to pass wind and instead he accidentally followed through in his pants.

DUNCAN SHEARER: At Huddersfield, Peter Ward would sit in the bath and tell everyone: "Here comes Tommy Turtle – he's going to poke his head out." Everyone would jump out the bath.

JIMMY SANDISON: I remember as the speeches started during a sports writers' dinner at the Hilton Hotel in Glasgow, John Martin was bursting for the toilet, but the big man – being ever so polite – didn't want to get up and disturb the speakers so he relieved himself into an empty wine carafe and placed it back on the table. I won't tell you if anyone sampled his vintage.

JOHN BURRIDGE: I used to travel from Durham every day and get the train to Waverley where I would have a motorbike chained up. I used to leave my helmet there. I was running late for training when I jumped on my bike and put my helmet on. As I was riding along Princes Street I could smell something funny. Someone had p****d in my bloody helmet.

MARCO MAISANO: After a night out at Morton, we came back to Chris Millar's place. Stewart Greacen is a big Rangers supporter and he found a pair of Celtic boxer shorts in Chris's bedroom. Stewart left a 'memento' in the boxers, wrapped them up and left them on the bed. Chris came in and knew instantly what had happened because the place stank.

ALLY MACMILLAN: I have to confess at Morton I let Dennis McGhee urinate in a ginger bottle and let Steve Aitken drink it.

DENNIS NEWALL: As a kid, I was working on a building site when I found a dead mouse and decided to put it in one guy's sandwich. The guy pulled out his lunch and was about to eat it when I lost my bottle and decided to tell him. He wasn't happy about the mouse but he still ate the sandwich after taking the mouse out and brushing the fluff away.

BRIAN MARTIN: St Mirren beat Rangers 1-0 at Ibrox the day they raised the championship flag. Frank McGarvey put his hand up to his ear to the Rangers fans after the game. It was around his birthday and there were cards and a present in a box for him at training on the Monday. It turned out some Rangers fan put dog s**t in a box for him.

PAUL LOVERING: The worst item of clothing I've ever seen is Craig McEwan's tight white cords. He came round to my house and sat on my couch when my Yorkshire Terrier Clea jumped on him. The dog farted on him but followed through. He went home with a big brown stain on his white trousers. Personally, I think the dog did him a favour.

RAY STEWART: Tony Gale was always playing jokes at West Ham. One time when he had piles he replaced Alvin Martin's toothpaste with his pile cream. I remember Alvin saying to Tony: "This toothpaste doesn't lather." That was hilarious. I never really fell victim that often – they wouldn't dare.

JOHN HILLCOAT: At St Mirren, someone urinated into an empty shampoo bottle and somebody else ended up using it on their hair. They were wondering why it wouldn't lather.

LEE WILKIE: When Ray Farningham was at Dens Park, he left a dead seagull in Paul Mathers' toilet bag. I don't think Paul was too happy and didn't speak to Ray for a couple of weeks.

NEIL BARRETT: At Dundee, Iain Anderson shaved the hairs of his legs and then sprinkled them into a chicken mayonnaise roll. Everyone then chipped in some money for Neil Jablonski to eat it. He ate it for about £100 but he ended up throwing most of it up.

EOIN JESS (Aberdeen): I have overlapping toes. My little toe on both feet hooks over on top of the next one. It has caused a lot of hilarity in every dressing room I've ever been in as they all think that I am a freak. Hey, maybe we've just found the key to why all my critics say I have never fulfilled my potential.

DANNY INVINCIBILE: In my first year at Swindon, a boy put a spud in Adam Willis' exhaust and the car backfired and got messed up pretty bad. About a week later Adam stuck a fish in with the radiator fluid of the poor boy's car. It was five days before he found it.

SCOTT ROBERTSON (Dundee, Dundee United): I was injured in a game against Ross County and got my testicles twisted. I went to hospital and I was placed in a room to have my bits scanned. Soon, a large group of doctors, nurses and students were crowding round my bed to have a look at a swollen, water-melon-sized mess between my legs. Everyone who had seen my injury at Dens soon spread the word and I was getting texts asking to me describe it. In the end I just sent them all a picture message of the damage. Some were sympathetic but there were plenty who weren't so kind-natured and found it more amusing.

STEVIE TOSH: When I was at Livingston, Graeme Coughlin used to be manky. Every game he used to go for a dump but he'd do it with the door wide open. No one needs to see that.

DEREK LILLEY (Morton, Dundee United): David Hopkin had false teeth. When he played, he didn't have them in, but there were times when he wasn't playing when he took them out to scare people. His favourite wind-up was when he was out in a pub or club, he'd stand next to someone and as soon as they looked away, or put their drink down, he'd whip out his falsers and put them in their glass. I know people who've emptied their glasses before noticing what's sitting at the bottom.

RAY FARNINGHAM: We were on holiday in Tenerife with Dundee during the 1993-94 season. Jim Duffy was in his first stint as manager there and we were in the Caledonian Bar when he lined up sixteen Green Monster specials. The players took turns to down their drinks but when Noel Blake went for it, he didn't realise his glass was full of washing up liquid. I've never seen a black man go green before – and he had to go outside to throw up.

GILLIAN DONALDSON: Our kit-man Andy Bryan likes to sniff things. He has a massive collection of football programmes and whenever we get one for our game the first thing he does is open it up and smell it. I swear if you blindfolded him, he could probably tell you which programme it was – he is sad that way. He also sniffs his clean washing.

DENNIS NEWALL: There were a pair of underpants which had not been washed for three weeks which were kicking about the dressing room and one of the guys stuck them in another guy's training bag for him to take home. They were pretty awful.

ALAN ROUGH: Derek Whyte did something to my face while I was sleeping when we shared a room at Celtic. He did something which is too disgusting to mention. I also shared with Everton keeper George Wood when playing for Scotland at the Home Internationals. He used to carry magazines like *Playboy* and *Penthouse* – he was always escaping to the toilets and I'd never be able to get in.

STEVEN THOMSON (Falkirk, St Mirren): At Crystal Palace, Gareth Davies took John Salako's convertible and parked it under a tree. When John found his car, it was covered in bird s**t and full of all sorts. He wasn't too happy.

CHRIS MILLAR: We had a problem with mice at Morton and would set up traps to try and catch them, but Jim McInally would stick them in people's shoes and the bread bin. The physio John Tierney nearly had a heart attack when he went to get some bread and found one.

BRYAN GILFILLAN: Derek Townsley brought in some Easter eggs for the young lads to share. Dene Shields and I took the centre out of one of them and filled it with foam burst. We gave it to Greg Fleming who bit into it. He wasn't happy. It couldn't have tasted very nice.

ANDY DOWIE: We were on a night out in Inverness. Michael Gardyne did a No.2 in a urinal. Some bloke walked in and commented that someone had left a Mars Bar in it. I have a clip of it on my mobile phone.

STEPHEN SIMMONS: Someone at Dunfermline peed into one of the shower bottles. I'm not sure who has been caught out with it and if you are asking who did it, I couldn't possibly say but maybe it is Scott Thomson, Scott Wilson or Owen Morrison.

PAUL MATHERS: You always had to be on the lookout at Dundee with Ray Farningham, Gerry Britton and George Shaw around. We were in Morecambe when they decided to get a whole load of mice and rats from a pet shop and let them loose in Jim Hamilton and Neil McCann's room.

COLIN CAMERON: At Raith Rovers, we had these big massive baths and we would always try to get in them before Shaun Dennis did, otherwise you might have found things floating about in them.

CHRIS SWAILES: I was training with Oldham and spotted a huge dead rat on the pitch. It was the size of a dog. I picked it up and hid it under my top from the lads and then I chased the boys, including the manager and coaches. I can still smell the rat to this day.

JAMES WESOLOWSKI (Hamilton): I played with Jonny Hayes when I was on loan at Cheltenham Town. He once ate a £5 note and then two days later he showed us the £5 again. You can work that one out for yourself.

JIM MCALISTER: Jim McInally caught a mouse after setting some traps so one of the boys got hold of it and put it inside the pool table. Andy McLaren went to rack up the balls and pulled out the mouse when reaching for them – I have never seen anyone screech and s**t themselves so much in all my life.

ARTHUR NUMAN: Some of the Italians at Rangers would go to the toilet, clean their a**e in the sink, then wipe it with the hand towel – and hang it back up! It was a horrible habit. I remember Lorenzo Amoruso did that as did Sergio Porrini, the b*****ds!

MARCO AND FLAVIO PAIXAO (Hamilton): We were training when a seagull s**t on the shoulder of our goalkeeper. The coach stopped the session and everybody was on the ground laughing. It was such a hilarious moment and we will never forget it.

CRAIG CONWAY: I have a Boxer dog and one summer's day I took it down the park. Unbeknownst to me, he had eaten a pair of my girlfriend Kristy's tights the night before. I basically had to pull the undigested tights out his backside with my bare hands while a kids' football team and many others looked on. It wasn't pretty and it was pretty embarrassing.